SIMPLIFYING T'AI CHI

An Explanation for Beginners

Trevor Reynaert

Not a book about specific T'ai Chi form - just one written for newcomers to T'ai Chi to answer some of the many questions that they may have as they begin their journey........

2017 Edition

3rd Revision - 2017 *(D)*

© 2011, 2014, 2017 Crystal T'ai Chi (Forest of Dean) UK

All rights reserved. Other than research or short review, no part of this book may be reproduced, stored in a retrieval system or transmitted in any form (electronic, mechanical, photocopying, recording, or otherwise) without prior permission of the author.

www.crystaltaichi.co.uk

Book produced & published by Crystal Technical Publications UK

ISBN 978-1-9998411-0-2

Disclaimer

T'ai Chi and Qi Gong are a very safe form of exercise when it is taught and practised correctly. However, if you have any health conditions you should review them with your Doctor before starting your T'ai Chi journey. Readers who engage in these activities do so at their own risk.

The author, publishers, distributors and anyone involved with this book will not be held responsible in anyway whatsoever for any injury or consequence that may arise as a result of following instructions in this book.

ALWAYS PRACTISE SAFELY WITHIN THE LIMITS OF YOUR ABILITY.

However as you read on - you'll find that you're never really too old or infirm to practise a little T'ai Chi or Qi Gong.

About the Author

Trevor has practised T'ai Chi for over 30 years and is a registered TCUGB Instructor, a fully accredited traditional Sun style Instructor with the Deyin Taiji Institute, and an Affiliated Master Instructor with the AMAA. As well as teaching traditional styles, he has had 16 years experience of teaching Dr Paul Lam's T'ai Chi for Health Programs for Arthritis, Back Pain, Diabetes, Osteoporosis and Falls Prevention.

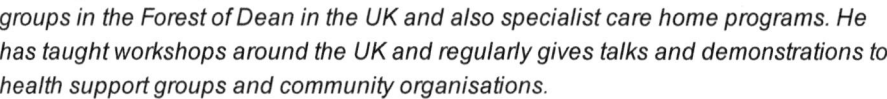

Trevor's passion is 'T'ai Chi for All Ages & Abilities', teaching several regular traditional and health T'ai Chi groups in the Forest of Dean in the UK and also specialist care home programs. He has taught workshops around the UK and regularly gives talks and demonstrations to health support groups and community organisations.

Trevor is a retired professional engineer and a Fellow of the Institute of Engineering and Technology. Following a 14 year technical and teaching career in the RAF, he then spent over 35 years travelling world-wide as a specialist engineering trainer and technical writer. His T'ai Chi journey started when he was In his late thirties, initially to manage and control his own chronic back problems. With health limitations of his own, he has found and developed an ability to empathise with others who have disabilities at any level.

In 2001, encouraged by meeting and training with Dr Paul Lam, Trevor formed Crystal T'ai Chi to pass on his personal experiences and the benefits that he obtained from T'ai Chi to people of any age or ability level, and since then he has fully endorsed all of Dr Lam's T'ai Chi for Health Programs which actively encourage mixed ability/age group sessions. Over the years he has also assisted Dr Lam as a trainer at UK leader workshops, and has had articles published on his website.

Trevor's early T'ai Chi training was in Yang style, but after studying and using modified Sun style forms to support health problems, his main focus turned to traditional Sun style T'ai Chi. After initially studying the form under Dr Paul Lam he has since been mentored and supported by Professor Li Deyin's daughter Faye Yip and other Sun style Masters who have been disciples of Sun Lutang's daughter, Sun Jian Yun. He practises and teaches traditional Sun hand forms (the original 97 step long form, Sun Jian Yun's 42 step, Deyin 13 and 38 step, and the 73 step competition form). Additionally he also practises and teaches the 108 step Long Yang style hand form that started his T'ai Chi journey many years ago, together with Jian (sword), Dao (sabre) and Shan (fan) forms. Qi Gong also plays a major role in all his teaching.

In 2009 Trevor created his own modified program (Twilight T'ai Chi) based on T'ai Chi and Qi Gong movements that he uses with great success with the elderly in care homes, many suffering from dementia and other age-related illness.

www.crystaltaichi.co.uk

Acknowledgements

There have been many T'ai Chi friends, teachers and students who have helped me with my own journey. It is impossible to name them all but my heartfelt thanks go to everyone who has supported me over the years and to those who continue to help me in future years. I must however give special thanks to the following, without whom I'm sure I would not have advanced so far:

The unknown Chinese gentleman - who after a chance meeting in Hong Kong many years ago spent several hours introducing me to basic posture.

Dr Paul Lam - whose personal encouragement and modified T'ai Chi programs for health have inspired me and given me the confidence and ability to teach and encourage others on their T'ai Chi journey.

Dr Paul Lam's master trainers - who have taught me standard and modified forms over the years.

Faye & Tary of the Deyin Taiji Institute - who have taught me advanced forms and inspired me in later years, taking my T'ai Chi to a higher level.

Joan Towell - who has assisted and supported me since I started teaching T'ai Chi, and who also helped verify the contents of this book.

Ken Hitchings - my wise old sage and neighbour - who has been a source of encouragement and help to me over the past 38 years.

Everyone who has allowed me to learn from them or to teach them - without them I would not have progressed as a teacher and so be motivated to study more.

The Care Homes - such as Hazelhurst and others local to me, where I have learnt that T'ai Chi has something to offer everyone no matter how frail they may seem.

The many, many authors of instructional books and videos - who have provided sources of reference over the years, especially *Tim Cartmell* for his translation of Sun Lu Tang's book, *Bill Douglas* for providing the simplified explanations that I needed when I started teaching and *Gerde Geddes* whose long Yang form video provided a basic visual reference in my early T'ai Chi years.

All those that have contributed to this book in other ways:

Ken, Norman, Jill, Margaret, Jean - and others (some alas no longer with us) who have allowed their pictures to be published.
Gill - my supportive wife.
Geoffrey - my photographer; *Carole* - my editorial proofreader; *Sheila Barbour, Margaret Billingham* - and other T'ai Chi colleagues who have critically reviewed my book before publication.

Contents

Disclaimer i
About the Author ii
Acknowledgements iii
Prologue 5

Chapter 1 The Art of T'ai Chi 7

What is T'ai Chi? 7
Origins of T'ai Chi 7
T'ai Chi – A Martial Art or an Exercise? 8
    Martial Art - Soft or Hard - Internal or External? 9
    T'ai Chi as Exercise 9
T'ai Chi is Fun 10

Chapter 2 The Healthy Side 11

T'ai Chi for Health 11
What's special about T'ai Chi Movement? 11
Age and Ability 12
Meditation in Motion - Swimming in Air 13
Examples of Proven Health Benefits 14
    Arthritis 14
    Back Pain 14
    Diabetes 15
    Osteoporosis 15
    Falls Prevention 15
    MS 16
    Stress 16
    General Age-related Conditions 16
T'ai Chi or Yoga? 17
    Similarities 17
    Differences 17

Chapter 3 T'ai Chi or Qi Qong? 19

A Confusing Name 19
What is Qi (Chi)? 19
    How do I feel it? 20
What is Qi Gong (Chi Kung)? 21
The Deeper Power of Qi Gong 22
How is Qi Gong Related to T'ai Chi? 22
    Qi Gong & Martial T'ai Chi 23
    Qi Gong & Health T'ai Chi 23
Types of Qi Gong 24

Chapter 4 Your T'ai Chi Teacher 27

I teach - I learn 27
Sifu 28
Your teacher 28

Chapter 5 Choosing Your First Class 31

What Style Do I Start To Learn? 31
    Yang Style 31

　　　　Sun Style 32
　　　　T'ai Chi Forms Modified For Health 33
　　　　Just Qi Gong - Not T'ai Chi 35

Chapter 6 Before You Begin 37

　　　　What Do I Wear? 37
　　　　Best Time & Place 37
　　　　Impromptu T'ai Chi 38
　　　　The T'ai Chi Salute 39
　　　　Do's & Dont's 41
　　　　After Your First Lessons 42

Chapter 7 Introducing a Few Words You'll Meet 45

　　　　The Terminology of T'ai Chi 45
　　　　　　'Allegorical' and 'Real' terms 45
　　　　　　Spelling - Western or Pin Yin? 46
　　　　What do you mean by .....? 46

Chapter 8 Getting Started 55

　　　　The Rooted Tree 55
　　　　Basic Posture 56
　　　　　　General Body Posture 57
　　　　　　A Relaxed Posture 57
　　　　　　The Head and Neck 58
　　　　　　The Chest and Back 59
　　　　　　The Legs 59
　　　　　　The Feet 60
　　　　　　The Knees 60
　　　　　　The Shoulders and Arms 61
　　　　　　The Hands 61
　　　　　　The Mouth 62
　　　　　　The Eyes 62

Chapter 9 How To Achieve Posture & Movement 65

　　　　The Basic Starting Posture 65
　　　　Weight Shift 68
　　　　Stepping Forward & Backward 70
　　　　Knee Movements 74
　　　　Simple Turns 76
　　　　Kicks 79
　　　　Kua 81
　　　　Transferring From A Low To A High Stance 83

Chapter 10 T'ai Chi Harmony 85

　　　　Breathing 85
　　　　　　Lower Abdominal Breathing 86
　　　　　　The Philosophy of Deep Breathing 86
　　　　Yin & Yang 87
　　　　Six Harmonies 89
　　　　　　Three External Harmonies 89
　　　　　　Three Internal Harmonies 90
　　　　　　The Six Harmonies Together As One 91

Silk Reeling Harmony 92
   Silk Reeling and Spiralling Energy 92
   Can a Beginner Develop Spiralling Energy? 94
The Harmony of Five Elements 94
   The Message Five Elements Gives to Beginners 96
Five Steps & Eight Energies (13 Postures) 97
   Five Steps 97
   Eight Energies 98

Chapter 11 Maxims For Enjoyable Safe Practice 101

General Movement Maxims 101
   Focused and Calm – Empty Mind 101
   Relaxed and Soft 102
   Concentration 102
   Slowness 102
   Spontaneity and Natural Movement 103
   Coordination 103
   Rooted and Sunk 103
   Balance 104
   Empty and full 104
Summary of Best Practice 105

Chapter 12 Introductory Practice 107

Just To Get You Started 107
   A Quick Reminder 107
Warming Up 109
Cooling Down 110
A Simple Introductory Qi Gong 111
A Simple Static Qi Gong '5 Element' 112
   Five Element Qi Gong Movement Sequence 113
   Five Element Qi Gong As A Simple Form 118
A Few Basic Sun Style Movements 119
   Introductory Sun Form Movements 120
A Few Basic Yang Style Movements 130
   The 8 Step Yang Form 130

Chapter 13 An Introduction To Zhan Zhuang 137

Standing Like A Tree 137
Before You Begin Zhan Zhuang 138
   Important Practice Tips Before You Start 139
The Postures Of Zhan Zhuang 141
   Commencing 141
   First Posture - Wu ji (the primary energy posture) 142
   Second Posture - Embracing the Tree 143
   Third Posture - Holding the Belly 144
   Fourth Posture - Standing in the Current 145
   Fifth Posture - Holding a Ball in Front of the Face 146
   Finishing the Session 146
Sequencing the Basic Postures 147

Chapter 14 A Potted History of T'ai Chi 149

Chen Style 151

- Yang Style 151
- Hao Style (Wu Hao Style) 155
- Wu Style 155
- Sun Style 156
- Lee Style 157
- Modified T'ai Chi for Health 158

Epilogue **161**

Index **163**

Prologue

This book is based on a series of notes that I originally wrote for those attending my T'ai Chi classes for health improvement. It is intended to introduce complete beginners and novices to the basic concepts and maxims of T'ai Chi and introductory Qi Gong. Hopefully the simplified content will answer questions, reassure, dispel misconceptions, and help novices progress along what is undoubtedly a rewarding road.

It is not intended to teach specific T'ai Chi form or replace the many existing in-depth books on form and technique that have been written by other formally trained masters and teachers.

The intended purpose is only to provide a documented reference of introductory information. Its content is based on the many questions that we are asked and general discussion that we have with our own beginners.

I have been teaching T'ai Chi for a number of years, have met and trained with many people and read many books on the subject. It's this combination that has provided me with a wealth of information that I want to pass on to others.

So please don't read this book and say 'this has been said before by so-and-so', or 'he read this in such-and-such a book'. In reality you may be right - but surely that is the mandate of any teacher - to read, observe and listen, and then pass on the knowledge he has gained. Please don't criticise the simplicity of the movement detail as being only superficially descriptive and lacking the full internal or martial intent - they are written for those of any ability who are starting their journey.

Do please accept the explanations in this book as my interpretation and contribution to introducing T'ai Chi to as many people as possible.

Trevor Reynaert 2014

Re-issued 2017 edition

As my 70th birthday approaches I have re-visited this book to make a few subtle changes to the original pictures and text, and have also added a new section introducing the beginner to the meditation and body control of Zhan Zhuang.

Currently the world around me is torn with turbulence, extremism and hatred. I'm sure that I'm not alone in wishing that the friendship, the harmonies of emotion and the control that T'ai Chi develops in us could be shared and practised by everyone to bridge the barriers created by religion and politics and produce a more peaceful future world.

Trevor Reynaert 2017

This book is dedicated to my wife Gill who has always been so supportive throughout my T'ai Chi endeavours.

"We have so many things worth learning, but knowledge is unlimited and life is limited, so even in our whole life we cannot finish our studies. Life begins at seventy! .....Everything is beautiful! Health is a matter of utmost importance, and all the rest is secondary. Now we must find out how to enjoy excellent health in our whole life."

T.T. Liang (Liang Tung-Tsai, 1900-2002)

Chapter 1
The Art of T'ai Chi

What is T'ai Chi?

T'ai Chi is now generally categorised in the western world as a "healthy exercise" and is increasing in popularity, but what is it?

There are many misconceptions about T'ai Chi and many questions that someone embarking on their journey of exploration will need answering.

- Is it a martial art? If so, what is its intent? Is it aggressive, or is it purely defensive?
- Is it a just a gentle exercise? If so does it have any intent or is it just aerobic?
- How is it practised today? How does it differ from other martial art or exercise programs?
- Does it have additional or less health benefits than those that are achieved with normal exercise programs?
- Do I have to start when I'm young or can anyone of any age gain benefit by starting? Do I have to be fit, agile and supple to start?
- Does it take long to learn? How long do I have to practise to gain benefit?

Hopefully by reading on, the answers will fall into place and you'll be able to enjoy and advance your T'ai Chi and see for yourself the improvements that it will bring to your life.

Origins of T'ai Chi

T'ai Chi has its origins rooted in Taoist philosophy. The basic concepts are alleged to have developed in Northern China around 1000 years ago during the Sung dynasty (AD960-1279).

The misunderstanding of many is that T'ai Chi as generally practised today is only the adoption of the training routines from the Chinese martial art T'ai Chi Chuan, with an emphasis on posture and movement improvement combined with an inner calmness and control. This is true in many cases but there are still many who learn and teach it as a true martial art.

The early years and techniques of T'ai Chi Chuan are cloaked with secrecy, partly because as a martial art, the safe keeping of technique was essential to maintain advantage, and partly because of the Chinese/Asian traditional ideology of Masters reserving knowledge to those of proven loyalty. Teaching was restricted to family (usually implying a village) or selected students, and passed down by word of mouth with nothing documented.

During the late 19th century and early 20th century, books and photographs of T'ai Chi styles and practice started to appear, with early movie clips following around 1930. The Chinese/Western amalgamation in Hong Kong and Singapore, combined with migration of Chinese culture to Taiwan and other south-east Asian countries encouraged the spread further.

For those who want to learn a little more you can find a very brief summary of key historical information later in this book on page 149.

T'ai Chi – A Martial Art or an Exercise?

One of the first things that I like to explain to all new students, both the young and fit and the older and less able, is to alleviate any confusion and/or misconceptions about whether T'ai Chi is an exercise regime or a martial art.

When you watch what has become the accepted practice of T'ai Chi form, it seems completely divorced from a fighting martial art. In some respects this is true. However, the forms are the basis of a training regime that was created to attain fitness combined with perfect body control and a calm but focused mind – the ideal requirements for those whose job it befalls to defend against aggression. These slow movements of the form however are deceptive as with further training each can be progressed if so desired into a fast, effective defensive action.

My classes are based upon using T'ai Chi for its health benefits. I'm sure that although most of the younger, fitter members appreciate that they are learning the prequel to a formal martial art, those who are past their prime, have had hip replacements, are disabled or wheel-chair bound, haven't come along to learn defensive applications! This doesn't mean, however, that actions and application are never analysed and are ignored. As progress is made, and where suitable, a generalised description of movement application is given and this encourages the person to better appreciate posture control and energy movement (intent). This provides for a safer and more effective practice.

Each action in T'ai Chi must have a purpose, whether described allegorically or by using a more descriptive martial term. As you will discover as you read on, T'ai Chi is not just aerobic movement.

Martial Art - Soft or Hard - Internal or External?

The series of continuous, slow, smooth and graceful moves of the form, supplely executed in a relaxed manner, and combined with an upright, balanced, rooted posture, form the basis of the T'ai Chi art.

This supple movement without apparent tension in the upper body leads to the categorisation of T'ai Chi as a 'soft' or 'internal' martial art. This is established against the practice of the 'hard' or 'external' martial art regimes exemplified by some of those taught by Wing Chun, Shaolin and other 'Kung Fu' schools.

These 'hard' fighting disciplines emphasising forceful, rapid, staccato moves executed with strength and power, often with locked joints, are more aggressive in approach. The more power, speed and accuracy that the person is able to concentrate in a movement, the better is its effective execution.

So how can T'ai Chi, a 'soft' art, be considered as being able to withstand the devastating power of exponents of the 'hard' school?

The key factor is that by practice of forms, a T'ai Chi exponent is very strong and very supple. Strength is concentrated in the legs which are solidly "rooted" to the ground, enabling a relaxed torso which is yielding and apparently 'soft'. Any force directed to the body will be dissipated as, effectively, there is no solid surface to absorb its energy. The aggressor finds that he is unable to focus his attack and vent the full force of his power, and the T'ai Chi opponent escapes maximum injury in the event of contact.

However, major contact is rare as the leg strength and suppleness of the T'ai Chi exponent allow a reaction like a coiled spring, recoiling away and avoiding any strong aggressive force, before springing back to counter-attack or block further aggression when that force is removed. The stronger the attacking force, the tighter the spring and the stronger the counter-attack.

The analogy often used compares the body during T'ai Chi practice to a tree. The legs are the trunk of the tree, rooted to the ground, with the arms and upper body flexible, supple and strong forming the branches. The branches flow and move gently resisting the wind, whilst the tree remains solidly supported by its rooted trunk.

T'ai Chi as Exercise

So how does practising the T'ai Chi form develop such strength and suppleness? The answer is by learning and practising the slow, flowing yet methodical movements of the form.

For the relatively fit and able, the meticulous, consistent repetition of a predetermined set of flowing arm and torso movements, made with the body relaxed and for the most part performed with the body upright and the back straight, strengthens the legs and loosens the upper part of the body. As we will discuss in more detail later, relaxation promotes the transfer of body weight to the legs. The more you can relax, the greater the weight that sinks down to your legs.

Movements are split into two parts, a Yin and a Yang component. As we make each movement pair, deep breathing provides a constant control similar to a metronome. This controlled breathing provides internal massage for heart muscles and inner core support muscles.

Appearances are deceptive. Despite its apparent effortlessness to the casual observer, when taught and practised correctly, each individual will be putting in considerable effort. Typical pulse rate increases from a resting 70 per minute to 120 per minute after just 7 minutes of practice have been recorded.

Completion of each movement sequence of the form stimulates the mind. 'What comes next?' The mind is therefore also exercised as more and more movements are added to the form.

T'ai Chi practice is therefore a complete Mind & Body exercise.

But what about those who are disabled or seated – how can they sink weight to the legs or move their upper body with suppleness? The answer lies in the way that T'ai Chi is taught.

The mind controls the arms and legs, and the arms and legs indicate back to the mind what the next movement is. Those disabled or seated can imagine that they are moving the same amount as those who are more able. The intent of the movement is transmitted through the body and the same balance will establish itself, usually with noticeable improved movement of any relatively mobile limbs.

As you read further, more of how and why will become apparent.

T'ai Chi is Fun

Yes, T'ai Chi is a serious activity, and to become proficient in its disciplines takes years of regular practice. However learning and practising T'ai Chi for health should be fun. Whatever level, if you become a member of a well run group with a good and understanding teacher, you will be put at ease from the beginning and the learning will be enjoyable with a sense of great achievement, and the practice, be it on your own or in the group, will be fun.

Chapter 2
The Healthy Side

T'ai Chi for Health

The majority of those who practise T'ai Chi today do so mainly for the benefits it gives as an exercise. In comparison, few learn it only for its martial aspects. As an exercise, if taught correctly, T'ai Chi is suitable for people of all ages and ability.

By applying the concepts and principles of the original martial art, T'ai Chi practice will stimulate blood circulation, improve breathing and loosen and gently exercise joints, while simultaneously promoting relaxation, relieving stress and encouraging an active mind. Using T'ai Chi to improve the body's metabolism and its general well-being, encourages the often untapped powers of self-healing. T'ai Chi practised diligently, will certainly help to manage and alleviate many medical conditions.

> *The purpose of T'ai Chi is to condition the mind by exercising the body and to exercise the body under motivation of the mind - to train the body without strain and cultivate the mind without tension. It is not intended to build big muscles, but to harmonise the mind and body for integration of total health. ...You may practise either the whole of T'ai chi Chuan or any part of it according to your convenience and endurance, but in order to achieve lasting benefits you must make it a daily task throughout your life......*
>
> *Master Liu Yao-Ting (1890 - 1984)*

Always view things in correct perspective though.
 T'ai Chi is not a universal panacea, but it will produce rewards that reflect tenfold the effort put into its practice.

But don't be too cynical either. More and more clinical studies are being carried out and modified T'ai Chi programs such as those by Dr Paul Lam are becoming universally accepted by the western medical profession.

What's special about T'ai Chi Movement?

It is said that the basic movement concepts of the soft martial arts such as T'ai Chi were created by observation of animal movements, hence the names that are used to describe some of the individual postures and movement sequences.

Consider a cat hunting, the smooth stalking and the dynamic pounce for the kill. No wasted energy or effort, just perfect body control. Consider the way that a standing stork or crane slowly spreads its wings, one up one down, or the smooth undulating advance of a snake.

The qualities of fitness, alertness, reaction and mental control are definitely required for an effective martial art, but are equally beneficial to help fight *dis-ease* and the traumas that life brings.

By behaving like the animals above and employing their skills of awareness, assessment, smoothness and control to perform a complete action, whether in a martial or general health sense, a T'ai Chi practitioner will be optimising his body movement and balance, maintaining reserves, and avoiding actions that may be potentially damaging such as uncontrolled twists and falls.

Age and Ability

When teaching T'ai Chi for health purposes, we are not attempting to produce unstoppable martial movement, but to introduce the basics and sound concepts of T'ai Chi in the hope that benefit will be gained by all who join in, enjoying the practice as their health or ability dictate.

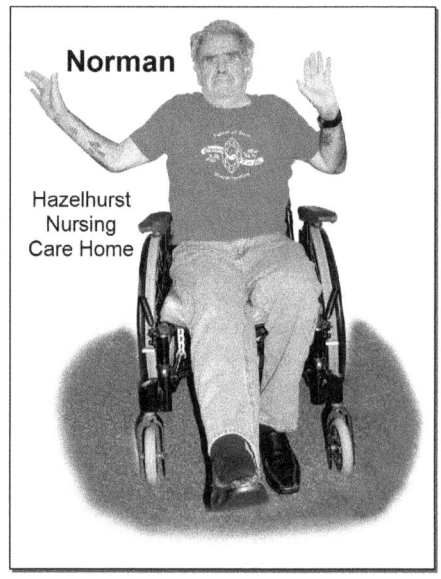

Norman

Hazelhurst Nursing Care Home

T'ai Chi is a very good form of exercise, particularly for the older age groups. The youngest I have taught has been 3 years old and the oldest 105!

T'ai Chi is not limited to the able either. I have taught several with severe disability - many wheelchair bound after a serious accident or stroke. In many of our normal sessions there are often seated members, and often this can be an excuse for everyone to sit to enjoy form in this way.

I have also developed a program based on basic T'ai Chi and Qi Gong movements that I use with groups of people suffering from dementia. The response and interaction achieved when compared to normal 'movement and exercise' sessions is truly amazing.

Chapter 2 The Healthy Side 13

Enjoying T'ai Chi & Qi Gong - Seated or Standing

Meditation in Motion - Swimming in Air

One of the unique features when using T'ai Chi as an exercise is that it promotes mental relaxation during movement. Calmness prevails with mental tensions focused but relaxed. We have Meditation in Motion.

T'ai Chi becomes a way of life........ No, I don't mean our lifestyle changes to one of alternate meditation/martial practice. What happens is that the calmness and controlled focused movement becomes a way of life. We think rationally and each movement is mapped out subconsciously before it is made. We Swim in Air.

  Steps are careful, smooth and balanced, minimising trips and falls.
  Strong leg muscles provide support for hip and knee joints, minimising wear.
  Movements are controlled.

These maxims follow into daily life where it becomes second nature to avoid making any spontaneous, jerked actions that could potentially cause subsequent damage to spine, hips, knees etc.

Once adopted, the same calmness takes over in everything we do. For example in verbal argument we allow the 'opponent' to vent his anger, gently deflecting it and allowing it to pass around us, until that is, a weakness is spotted, and we deliver a devastating well-metered counter-attack response.

Examples of Proven Health Benefits

There are many proven studies that now positively show the benefits a T'ai Chi exercise program can bring, many of which have modified forms associated with them.

Health benefits not only apply to a lifetime's practice, but reflect on any age that T'ai Chi is started.

You're never too old to start to practise T'ai Chi for health reasons. Find a teacher who is sympathetic to the frailty of age and medical conditions and start to benefit. Any effort you put in will be rewarded tenfold.

Here are some examples of how T'ai Chi can be used to assist in the health management of common chronic ailments.

Arthritis

The gentle relaxed movement of T'ai Chi practised with no tension and loose open joints, encourages overall blood flow and also the movement of synovial fluid, lubricating the painful joints, reducing pain a little which in turn encourages further movement.

There have been several clinical studies carried out on using T'ai Chi to help arthritis. Using Dr Paul Lam's modified Sun Form, a randomised study conducted by a collaboration of two universities and a hospital and published in 2003, reported that the condition showed an improvement in movement and pain relief by 29-35% within three months.

In this group of older women with Osteoarthritis, the arthritic symptoms, balance, and physical functioning was greatly improved. Patients had 35% less pain, 29% less stiffness, 29% more ability to perform daily tasks (such as climbing stairs), as well as improved abdominal muscles and better balance.

This study is typical of many other testimonials.

Back Pain

Gentle modified T'ai Chi programs for health such as the one used for Arthritis, can be practised seated or standing. In both of these positions, the basic corrected posture corrects one of the common causes of back pain.

Also the movement and balance aspects, combined with encouraged deep breathing, strengthens the deep stabilising core muscles of the back. These deep muscles close to the spine stabilise and protect it, and so strengthening them will help reduce pain and improve physical function.

Diabetes

T'ai Chi exercises the cardio-pulmonary system. As well as a general health benefit, this type of gentle exercise is particularly beneficial for those with type 1 or type 2 diabetes, as too is the calming stress-relief achieved.

Another less obvious benefit is the improved awareness of foot movement and balance that is enormously helpful to those with this condition, as foot de-sensitivity is a common side-effect.

Osteoporosis

As age takes its toll, this condition affects the majority of the population - not just the ladies. Although normally associated with post-menopausal women, it equally affects men. This condition reduces bone density and greatly enhances the possibility of fractures from even a small fall.

Controlled clinical studies have shown that there is a significant slowing down of bone density decline and an improvement in balance in older adults when T'ai Chi is practised regularly. In addition the general reduction in stress and improvement to quality of life that T'ai Chi can give will provide further benefit to help combat the effect of osteoporosis.

When first diagnosed, many people immediately metaphorically wrap themselves in cotton wool, fearing exercise, crowds or even just going out, due to a perceived fall, accident or stress fracture. This is the start of a vicious downward spiral - lack of exercise and fear exasperate the condition. T'ai Chi can provide the gentle exercise, minimise falls (see next) and inspire confidence and balance.

Please note that due to the possibilities of stress fractures, not all T'ai Chi forms are suitable for those with osteoporosis. Beginners should always start with a gentle modified form taught by a teacher who is aware of the potential associated problems.

Falls Prevention

T'ai Chi is highly effective as a prescribed exercise program for falls prevention for older people.

Learning the balanced movement of T'ai Chi helps provide the stability that is essential as we loose agility. It also improves confidence which in itself produces better mobility.

T'ai Chi can additionally combat the withdrawal that is often bought on by the fear of falling. By incorporating socialising with a sense of achievement, anyone loosing self-confidence will be encouraged to a significant improvement in quality of life!

Surprisingly comparison studies have shown that classic exercises such as swimming and walking do not significantly reduce the risk of falling for older people as T'ai Chi does. Of course, swimming and walking are still wonderful exercises in their own right.

MS

Exercise is an essential part of many approaches to controlling conditions like Multiple Sclerosis where the body's spontaneous reaction to movement requests is severely curtailed.

The slow movement and balance control of T'ai Chi becomes a valuable aid for those with MS, where the demands of normal exercise may have become unachievable and stressful.

Modified T'ai Chi programs with added Qi Gong, practised seated or standing, have proved very successful as a gentle exercise routine for those with MS.

Stress

One of the key features of T'ai Chi and Qi Gong practised for health is the generated calmness that coined an alternative name *Meditation in Motion*.

For those suffering from stress and its associated anxieties, allowing Qi Gong and simple T'ai Chi to enter into their life will definitely prove to be a positive benefit. It will improve their mind, help relaxation and improve mental strength so they can better cope with perceived problems.

The same also applies to those suffering with other chronic medical conditions. They are very likely to be mentally stressed and depressed because of an increasing inability to function normally on a day-to-day basis.

T'ai Chi is equally beneficial to combat the low level stress of life in modern society. We all experience this to one degree or another, and a little Qi Gong seated at our desk or when the kids are playing, or a short practice during the lunch break, can liberate new energy and turn a bad day around.

General Age-related Conditions

As already discussed T'ai Chi can improve conditions that develop with age such as arthritis, osteoporosis and diabetes.

It can be used for falls prevention programs and can also very effectively help those with strokes, Parkinson's - even dementia, and improves immunity, etc. etc....

More importantly, remember T'ai Chi can be fun and significantly improves quality of life!

T'ai Chi or Yoga?

I'm often asked to compare T'ai Chi and Yoga. I know many teachers who teach Yoga and many who teach both. I have several students who practise both. I have several students who have stopped Yoga and turned to T'ai Chi, and I'm sure that there are some who have done the reverse.

T'ai Chi and Yoga are complementary disciplines, and your T'ai Chi practice may prepare you to dip your toe into Yoga, or vice versa. Both have their unique strengths.

Similarities

- Both T'ai Chi and Yoga share a similar pedigree and origin.
- Both are excellent mind and body fitness regimes.
- Both help us let go of stress and cultivate a sense of well being in our lives.
- Both can be very gentle and, taught correctly, be used by almost anyone.

Differences

- T'ai Chi movement is more easily practised than Yoga by those in wheel chairs.
- T'ai Chi continually challenges our balance in a way that is applicable to everyday motion, whereas Yoga tends to be more static with many postures lying down.
- T'ai Chi can be practised spontaneously anywhere, outdoors or in, and wearing general clothing (ideal for workplace/office breaks).
- While Yoga postures are often static, T'ai Chi's postures flow one into the other, just as life's changes flow, making it an ideal lifestyle model.
- While Yoga is practised to prepare the body to experience a blissful meditative state, with T'ai Chi, the Qi Gong meditative state is often practised before movements, or in other words the ideal of T'ai Chi is to bring the state of enlightened awareness into our physical lives.

Yoga takes you to a place of peace
T'ai Chi brings that place of peace to you

This is a book about T'ai Chi. I practise and teach T'ai Chi - but both T'ai Chi and Yoga are wonderful disciplines with their own plus points. So if you are in doubt try both, make your decision, and maybe do both. Whatever the outcome I'm sure it will be rewarding for you.

CHAPTER 3
T'AI CHI OR QI QONG?

To the Chinese 'If you don't have Qi you must be dead'

So far we've been talking mainly about T'ai Chi, although you may have noticed several references to Qi Gong (Chi Kung) - *normally pronounced as 'chee gong'* - in earlier parts of this book. Most people who are learning or who teach T'ai Chi will include this in their practice to provide powerful internal and external exercise routines.

The subject of Qi Gong *(Chi Kung)* and of Qi *(Chi)* warrants much more coverage than the brief introduction that I am providing next. However, I hope that this will suffice for a beginner and be enough to satisfy initial curiosity, triggering further investigation to discover the potential power that it brings.

A Confusing Name

Before we look at what Chi Kung is let's talk about the name. Unfortunately a confusion arises with the word 'Chi', which we have already used in the expression 'T'ai Chi' *(Tai Ji)*, and now are using in 'Chi Kung' *(Qi Gong)*.

The Chinese words of 'Ji' and 'Qi' are both pronounced and written in the western way as 'Chi' *(chee)* but have different meanings:
In the case of T'ai Chi *(Tai Ji)* the translation of 'Ultimate' applies to the word *Ji*. This gives us the definition of T'ai Chi Chuan as Grand or Supreme *Ultimate* Fist.
In the case or Chi Kung *(Qi Gong)* the translation of 'Breath' or 'Life Force Energy' applies to the word *Qi*.

To differentiate and to minimise confusion throughout this book I'll refer to 'Tai Ji' as 'T'ai Chi', and use the term 'Qi Gong' when referring to the energy exercises, and 'Qi' when referring to the energy itself.

What is Qi (Chi)?

Some say Qi is fictional, others say Qi is magic, Chinese culture says Qi is 'Life Energy'.

Looking at it with western simplicity as beginners let's start by thinking of it as 'breathing'. Once you have learnt to breathe deeply and correctly, with good posture and relaxed and open joints, you will start to experience real effects of Qi.

When I introduce the concept I say that Qi is in all of us just as are our five senses. Most of us have never consciously been made aware of it. A lack of knowledge for generations means most people never realise its presence, but to me it exists as a 'sixth sense'.

A general Chinese definition summarises it perfectly. It is in all living things and is in our body, in our blood, in our breath. It surrounds us in the air that provides that breath. It 'energises' us.

The Chinese Masters say that if you don't have Qi you must be dead!

Uncultivated Qi is the 'energy' that we often unconsciously feel but never really categorise. The warmth that radiates from a kind and loving person. The aggression that radiates from an enemy. The hardness that we sense when facing someone who doesn't care. The inner strength that we gain when faced with adversity. The subconscious warning of imminent danger.

Controlled and cultivated Qi is generated when we practise T'ai Chi correctly and is integral with true practice. That is why I feel that it is essential that the concept is at least considered by all who practise the art, whether in its martial form or as an exercise. Belief in its power is not essential but a general understanding and appreciation of its superficial effects are.

How do I feel it?

You will start to feel controlled Qi when you first learn to relax the body, achieve a generally more loose posture by opening the joints and start to focus on your breathing.

The usual sensation will be of a warmth or tingling in the extremities such as the fingers or toes. You won't feel Qi until you are relaxed and focused.

To those who don't want to delve deeper I always ask that they look at it as a basic western concept in that relaxed loose joints encourage and maximise the flow of blood that has been fully oxygenated by deep breathing - and just leave it at that.

For those of you who want to learn more, then as you start to practise Qi Gong and T'ai Chi, you will become more aware and initially feel it manifesting as an 'energy ball' that you can rotate, expand or compress between the hands.

Eventually, after practising you experience the ability to feel and control its movement around your whole body, spiralling it to add power to your movements. Your journey has begun. Now you can start to learn to fully master and use Qi, both internally and detecting it in others.

Deeper study leads into the link between meridian lines and movement of Qi along them. These meridians are serviced by the triggered points that are used by acupuncturists. In this context, focused Qi (and the associated Qi Gong exercises) can be seen as a 'self-induced acupuncture'.

What is Qi Gong (Chi Kung)?

We have already defined *Qi* as 'Life Energy' with a start point as 'breath'. *Gong* is loosely translated as 'exercise or work' or the 'benefits gained from perseverance of the practice'.

Verbally passed down and documented for over three millennia, you will see Qi Gong performed all over China. When practised correctly it has powerful self-healing properties.

Qi Gong forms the basis of the health elements of your T'ai Chi and takes many guises. Your teacher will introduce it in many ways, which may include variants as a basic exercise or warm up, or as a healing deeper meditation.

Qi Gong is a lifetime's art in itself - you can study and practise it by exploring its inner depths in isolation, and many do. However, I think it is fair to say that you can practise Qi Gong very effectively and never visit T'ai Chi, but you cannot practise T'ai Chi without understanding the basic principles of Qi Gong. T'ai Chi is a martial art developed from basic Qi Gong movement.

Qi Gong can therefore be defined in two simple ways dependant upon our expectations and belief in its power:

- Breathing and fitness exercises.
- Working with life energy to control its distribution around the body to improve overall health and harmony.

The first definition is a reality to novices as it has a definable meaning. The second definition describes effects that are often immediately felt by the beginner, but which take lots of practising to master well.

We've all done it!

So you've never done any Qi Gong before? ... Yes you have.

Everyone unwittingly carries out a basic Qi Gong, usually several times a day ... Really?

You didn't sleep so well last night, you're feeling a little bored or maybe you just feel generally lethargic. How does your body react? ... You YAWN.

Yes ... a yawn fits the definition of Qi Gong exactly.

You expand the body and open the mouth to inhale slowly and deeply. Then you exhale slowly and relax the body creating a feeling of release and a wakening mild exhilaration. Often this repeats several times ... Qi Gong!!

Think about it - we've automatically retained this breathing exercise - but how many more Qi Gong actions have we lost or forgotten over the millennia?

The Deeper Power of Qi Gong

Qi Gong is a holistic (whole body) system of self-healing exercise and meditation. It is a very powerful and deep art that has evolved over many millennia, combining the disciplines of posture, movement, self-massage, breathing techniques, and meditation.

The intention is that by learning and practising these techniques, Qi is built up, moved and stored in the body. Any impure Qi - *dis-ease* - can also be cleansed and replaced by purer, healing Qi. The Chinese have long appreciated the healing and preventive powers of Qi Gong, and it is now regularly integrated with modern medicine as part of their treatment for most general and many serious conditions.

At its simplest, Qi Gong practice makes available the process of absorbing a pure source of energy (oxygen) and eliminating the impure (carbon dioxide) more efficient and beneficial. In turn this oxygenates and improves blood flow.

Whatever your opinions, Qi Gong and the management of Qi will certainly improve your breathing and cardio-vascular system.

Qi Gong, practised either on its own, or combined into a T'ai Chi form, is as enjoyable as any sport, and provides a great sense of well-being, but without requiring a great expenditure of time or money.

Anyone can practise Qi Gong and it is normally recommended that a daily effort for around 30 to 60 minutes should be aimed for. It can be adapted for every age and physical condition, either standing, seated, or lying down. This makes basic Qi Gong an ideal exercise for the disabled or elderly.

How is Qi Gong Related to T'ai Chi?

T'ai Chi and its training forms that are more popular today, are a martial art based on Qi Gong philosophy and movement. You can practise Qi Gong without T'ai Chi but you cannot practise T'ai Chi without at least understanding the basic principles of Qi Gong.

As you learn T'ai Chi you are using the same basic postures and stances as Qi Gong. However, T'ai Chi practice requires a stable rooted stance with the body balanced at all times. In this respect advanced Qi Gong practice starts to deviate as it can often involve demanding movements that do not always comply with the stability and response required in a martial art.

Qi Gong & Martial T'ai Chi

Each movement in T'ai Chi, whether in a practice form or as an application of martial force, has a related Qi movement and harmony.

Martial T'ai Chi detects an opponent's aggressive energy and either deflects it or expresses forceful energy in defence. For the defender, the nature of Qi-control maintains a calm demeanour whilst simultaneously harnessing a powerful store of strength.

Many traditional Qi Gong sequences require very supple movement and can involve some extreme positional movement which are excellent for improving body fitness and strength as well as mental attitude and internal energy awareness. An appreciation of Qi and of Qi Gong is therefore essential for training in the full martial art that is T'ai Chi Chuan.

Qi Gong & Health T'ai Chi

When T'ai Chi is practised as an exercise for health purposes it is very important that an individual's movement limitations are related to by the teacher and the pupil. These limitations apply equally to any Qi Gong practised to supplement the T'ai Chi forms.

It has been my experience, that due to the wide variety of Qi Gong styles available, it can sometimes happen that inappropriate sets incorporating excessive bending and extreme posture are used in sessions of health-related T'ai Chi.

This is detrimental, not just because of the use of postures that may potentially exacerbate further damage, but also, unless a person is relaxed and achieving without pain or fear of further injury, they will never experience the real intended effects.

Despite this, it is very important that some suitable Qi Gong routines are introduced into T'ai Chi sessions to gain an appreciation of Qi, and transforming the practice from an aerobic dance to a health-invoking and meaningful internal and external exercise. All the sessions and classes that are run by us contain at least 15 minutes of a variety of selected simple Qi Gong routines that can all be done seated if required.

Types of Qi Gong

There is definitive archaeological evidence of Qi Gong dating back to at least 600 BC and many will say earlier than that. However, beginners can simply relate to three basic types: Passive, Moving and Meditative.

Passive (Static) Qi Gong

Jean

Here the emphasis is on focussed controlled breathing using basic simple movement to stimulate internal energy. They are practised from a basic standing (or seated) position. These postures are deliberate, controlled and in some cases may be held for several minutes.

When observed these movements appear easy, but in reality they can be deceptively difficult to fully master in order to develop both outer strength with strong posture and inner calm.

Typical of these is the *Five Element Qi Gong* which you can find on page 112, or *Zuan Zhuang* which you can find on page 137.

Moving (Flowing) Qi Gong

In this type of Qi Gong, the basic static stance is initially adopted, but flowing extension and bending arm and body movements are added to promote physical exercise. Again the movement is focused and is matched by controlled breathing.

In their simple form the gentle movement can often be less demanding on legs, back and arms than the more stationary positions of the static type. However, the physical movement involved with many of these Qi Gongs can prove very strenuous as the exercise movement develops.

Practised gently and within moderation they are an excellent way to initially help you to unwind, relax and build up body strength prior to T'ai Chi form. Internally they 'pump' Qi around the body along the meridians and into all organs. The body becomes supple and any stiffness or tension is relieved.

Typical of these are the Qi Gongs such as *Eight Pieces of Brocade (Ba Duan Jin)* and *Five Animals Qi Gong.*

Meditative Qi Gong

This group of Qi Gong involves minimal external movement and has a primary use in stress management. Generally it is carried out lying down, seated or sitting cross-legged in an upright 'meditation' position. *An obvious T'ai Chi/Yoga link.*

There are various techniques but to generalise, as in other forms of meditation, the mind is cleared and, whilst focusing on breathing, an awareness of Qi energy is cultivated, stimulated and moved around the body.

CHAPTER 4
YOUR T'AI CHI TEACHER

I Learn so that I can Teach - I Teach so that I can Learn

It is a fact that few people today have sufficient motivation and the self-discipline to ignore the ever-persuasive attractions of modern society and undertake the years of painful practice and relative isolation essential for the complete mastery of T'ai Chi as a martial art. Relatively few people have therefore mastered the true depth of T'ai Chi and are able and willing to pass on their knowledge of it. Traditionally of those who do, few are willing to describe more than the basic factors on which it is based, and then only in very vague and general terms.

Even teaching T'ai Chi as a health exercise has limited appeal as it rarely provides a lucrative livelihood. The rewards are rich, but they are not the material ones expected by the majority today.

So what does it mean when I say that I teach T'ai Chi? Am I a martial art expert? Of course not. I teach T'ai Chi to learn T'ai Chi.

I teach - I learn

Let me first explore my personal reasons and philosophy for wishing to share my passion with as many as I can, and then also try to explain the principles that I adopt when teaching.

I was a product trainer in electronic/mechanical engineering for over 35 years and have worked around the world teaching people of all skill levels. Always I remained aware that I was training my peers. *We were all equals.*

When working with trainers and engineers, I knew that I was there because I had new information that others now needed in order to be able to do their job efficiently maintaining state-of-the-art equipment. For my part, in order to do my job well I had spent months questioning the design, production and assembly engineers responsible for conceiving and building the product. I had listened to their answers and used my skills to put together a suitable training package that I could pass on.

Very importantly I also knew that I must listen to those who in turn were hanging on every word that I said. I must give them the opportunity to question the information and techniques that I was imparting.

Often this would lead to an improved method of teaching a particular operation, or even product modification being suggested. There were also times when I would not have the specialist knowledge to fully explain the conceptional technicalities behind a particular process. Very often one of my peers would proffer the explanation I needed.

> *I, the teacher, was still questioning, listening and learning.*

A good teacher is receptive, listens to his students and learns from them. In return good teachers live on through their pupils.

In mid-life when I started my T'ai Chi journey, I came across many strict dogmatic 'teachers' who considered their role was to show, instruct, correct and criticise – but not listen and mentor. These teachers weren't for me.

Sifu

During my early T'ai Chi research I read an article about teaching T'ai Chi. Although its origins are faded in the mists of time, its words have remained with me since. At the risk of plagiarism, here's my own interpretation:

In martial arts those who teach are often called 'Sifu' or 'Shi-fu'. You will find that this is usually translated as 'master' and 'teacher', (or in esoteric terms 'spiritual father'). My preferred translation was provided by an elderly Chinese gentlemen I met many years ago who defined the term as *'a teacher who is always learning and teaching more'*.

Ironically I recently came across a much more modern definition in the technical anachronism SIFU which was defined as 'Special Interface Unit' - this seems just as appropriate!

I have always considered myself to be a maieutic teacher. Maieutic teachers are ones who helps to encourage and bring out concepts that are growing within their pupils. The maieutic maxim is that many important lessons and truths cannot be taught directly as a transmission of knowledge from an instructor to a learner, but instead the learner learns these truths by interacting with an instructor to stimulate his or her own experience. A student is not an empty vessel to be filled with the wisdom of the teacher, instead the teacher is like a midwife bringing a child that has been growing inside its mother into the light.

Your teacher

In the early days your T'ai Chi will only be as good as your teacher. Look for a good teacher. If you find one, learn as much as you can. Remember though, you are there to learn but your teacher loves to teach *and* learn.

Do not hesitate to query why a move should be made in a particular way or why a hand or a leg should be placed in just this position and not in another. The answer probably lies in the application of that move in a combat situation and often this is disguised by the slow and apparently meaningless action of the form.

It is not the intention in this book to delve into these deeper aspects, but your teacher should be capable of justifying the rights and wrongs of a particular posture. A bonus of understanding a little of the original intent of the movement is that you will achieve better posture and an additional mental trigger to help you remember the move.

Bear in mind too that it can often be difficult for a teacher to project him/herself into the mind of the learner, but your teacher should always empathise with you, and you with your teacher. Mutual respect and adaptivity to your needs are essential, and become even more important when teaching/learning T'ai Chi as an aid to health and well-being.

At first I take up T'ai Chi as a hobby,
Gradually I become addicted to it,
Finally I can no longer get rid of it.
I must keep practising for my whole life
- it is the only way to preserve health.

The more I practise, the more I want to learn
from teachers and books.
The more I learn, the less I feel I know.
The theory and philosophy of T'ai Chi is so profound and abstruse!
I must continue for ever and ever....
It is the only way to improve and better myself.

T.T. Liang (Liang Tung-Tsai, 1900-2002)

CHAPTER 5
CHOOSING YOUR FIRST CLASS

Once you have decided to learn T'ai Chi, look for a class to attend. Ideally try to find one that is local to you as having to travel a distance to and from sessions can soon become onerous and tiring.

It may be that you can find a short introductory workshop instead. Even though this may be a distance away it will be an ideal way to try T'ai Chi and experience a specific style.

What Style Do I Start To Learn?

There are several styles of T'ai Chi and many different forms within that style making it difficult to know where to start. The important thing is that you do indeed start to practise T'ai Chi and that you find a good teacher.

Having looked and found a potential class, talk to the teacher and find out more about the type and style that is taught, especially if you have an age or ability issue. If you are happy then give them a try. It is only then that you will see if your choice is suitable. If it isn't, then don't give up, keep looking and try somewhere else.

Let me offer my simple guide to the basic common styles and forms that you should look for as an average beginner. I practise and teach both Sun and Yang styles but my personal preference for beginners would be Sun style or Dr Lam's modified variants.

Other traditional styles such as Chen or Wu, can and do accommodate beginners, but the majority of you who are new to T'ai Chi will find them too demanding initially, and thus may be deterred from continuing.

Yang Style

Yang style is the most common one that is taught to beginners around the western world, estimated to be around ninety percent of classes. The style was created by Yang Lu-Ch'an in the mid 1800s.

Characterised by its rooted stance, its movements are gentle and graceful and suitable for all ages. I find the Yang form performed slowly is a perfect stress-relief tool. However for those with poor balance or knee/hip replacement, I always recommend Sun style.

Because of the popularity of Yang form, and thousands of global teachers over the past 50 years, the original traditional form has evolved many variants. Typically though, you will most likely come across the following standardised Yang style hand forms:

- The most commonly taught 24 step 'Short' Yang form, which takes around 6-8 minutes to perform. Created in the mid-1950s by the newly formed Chinese Sports Commission, it is sometimes referred to as the 'Beijing 24'.

- The traditional 'Long' Yang form, attributed to Yang Lu-Ch'an. which takes around 15 to 20 minutes to perform. This is often referred to as the '108 Step Yang', however the actual number quoted varies depending upon how the movements have been broken down and the steps counted (for example 103 or 85).

- Variants created during the twentieth century by other Masters such as Chen Man Ch'ing.

- An 8 Step version which was developed in 1999 by the official Chinese Sports Council and often used to teach the primary movements of Yang form. This is a compact form, and is an ideal way to learn basic movement and posture. The form takes around 4 minutes to complete, but with only one step sideways left and right, it is ideal for home practice in a small two metre space.

I have included the 8 Step version "A Few Basic Yang Style Movements" on page 130 in Chapter 12 to provide a basic introduction to Yang style.

Sun Style

Sun style T'ai Chi was the last major form style to be created. It has elements taken from other traditional T'ai Chi styles, plus elements of Ba Gua and Xing Yi martial arts, making it a more diversified form adaptable to mixed abilities and applications. This is my favourite and has become my signature style.

The form - often referred to as 'nimble T'ai Chi' - is characterised by its upright stance, agile steps and powerful internal and external movements. Unlike Yang style, generally whenever one foot moves forward or backward the other foot follows creating a flowing "lapping wave" effect. Easy on the knee joints, this form is particularly suitable for all age groups, and its therapeutic properties make it ideal for people with balance and joint problems. This attribute has been adopted by Dr Paul Lam who uses Sun form as the basis for his T'ai Chi for Arthritis and other modified forms for health (see later on page 33).

Typically you will most likely come across the following standardised traditional Sun style hand forms:

- The original traditional Sun 97 step Long Form devised by Sun Lu-tang in 1919 and a 42 step Short Form created by his daughter Sun Jian Yun.

- A Sun 73 step Competition Form sequence devised by a Wu Shu Committee for the first Asian games in 1991. This was based on the 97, with a few movements modified to test athletes' flexibility, stamina and control of balance.

- A traditional Sun 38 step Short Form developed by Professor Li Deyin (a member of the committee above) and a 13 step version developed by Professor Li's daughter Faye to introduce the form to beginners. This is an ideal compact form for newcomers to T'ai Chi in general or to Sun form, taking around two minutes to perform and requiring only just over two metres space, so it is easy to do at home.

For those wishing to try Sun style, I have included a sequence of few simpler movements from Sun forms in Chapter 12.

T'ai Chi Forms Modified For Health

This group of forms have been created by various experienced teachers to aid and help manage chronic medical and age-related conditions.

For Chronic Medical Conditions

If you are not so active and feel you are in this category don't be put off from learning T'ai Chi. Some of the most popular modified forms (and the ones that I whole-heartedly support) are those that have been developed by Dr Paul Lam, a Doctor of western medicine and the winner of several gold and silver medals for

T'ai Chi in Chinese International competition. Since the mid-1990s he has achieved world-wide recognition for these modified T'ai Chi programs for various health conditions, all of which have been fully medically researched.

Dr Lam's T'ai Chi for Arthritis *(Sun Style)*

T'ai Chi for Arthritis was Dr Lam's flagship program and has now been used successfully all over the world for many years. Based on Sun form, its aim is to increase mobility and balance as an aid to the management of arthritis.

I use this all the time as a signature form for classes containing older and less able people. It can also be used very effectively seated.

Other forms Dr Lam has developed, such as one for Osteoporosis and Falls Prevention, are based on a mixture of Sun and Yang styles.

For The Severely Disabled

Persons who are severely disabled, or older people who by necessity are living in residential and care homes, are increasingly being offered T'ai Chi as an activity. If you are one of them, or responsible for introducing activity to these places, then you should certainly try it.

Hazelhurst Nursing Care Home

Norman

I find that with empathy and encouragement from the right teacher, many of the modified health T'ai Chi and Qi Gong programs can easily be adapted to suit. Movements may not be accurately achieved, but as long as they are done safely they will still be very beneficial. Joints and muscles that are probably now rarely used will be stimulated and the cardiovascular system improved.

From a teacher's perspective, attention span and overall ability vary so much within such groups, and so it is important that the program should be fun and not appear too serious.

For several years now I have used my own *Twilight T'ai Chi* program which I developed to address the issues of integrating people with Alzheimer's into the groups. In this the movements are related to everyday activities which stimulates activity, interaction and fun. Part of this program involves using fans to provide focus and extend movement range.

For Children

Many traditional teachers will adopt the classic approach that children should be taught in the same way as adults to build up their skills. While I don't disagree with this, only a few will have the motivation and drive to use this route.

For the majority of younger children, the use of modified programs that have been developed to take into account age, attention span and the need for fun are more suitable. These are well worth exploring as they will progressively seed the T'ai Chi philosophy which will hopefully remain throughout life.

Just Qi Gong - Not T'ai Chi

Some of you may decide that you really only want to practise Qi Gong (explained on page 21), or may only be able to find a Qi Gong class. That's fine. Most of the information in this book applies equally to T'ai Chi and Qi Gong.

Remember, I have already said that you can practise Qi Gong very effectively and never visit T'ai Chi, but you cannot practise T'ai Chi without understanding the basic principles of Qi Gong. T'ai Chi is a martial art developed from basic Qi Gong movement.

Just as with T'ai Chi, there are many different types of Qi Gong, some gentle and some very demanding, with very active movement (unlike the simple one that I have provided in this book on page 112) - but all demand the same basic internal and external maxims to provide safe movement and inner energy flow.

Chapter 6
Before You Begin

So you've found a teacher and class and have an idea of the style that you are about to learn. This chapter will offer answers to some of the general questions that a beginner often asks when about to start attending their first T'ai Chi session.

What Do I Wear?

Although there is traditional T'ai Chi clothing available, these are usually kept for special or demonstration events. Most of us normally practise in general casual wear.

Shirts tend to consist of a loose-fitting, sweat-absorbing polo shirt or tee shirt.

Trousers or skirts should definitely be of a loose 'sports' type, essential to permit free leg movement when graduating to kicks. Baggy cotton martial art trousers are a worthwhile investment as (politely) they have generously extended gussets to permit adventurous kicks without the danger of an embarrassing split seam.

Avoid using skin-tight pants and shirts during practice. As well as restricting movement they restrict the loose open posture we try to achieve and can also impede blood and Qi flow.

Shoes are another essential. When you are practising your T'ai Chi form you should always wear a pair of flat-soled lightweight shoes to "feel" the ground and avoid injury to your soles. (Bare feet are not recommended by most teachers as feet need support, and also because most practice areas cannot be guaranteed to be debris free.) Heavyweight shoes or trainers should be avoided as they tend to impede foot and leg balance and give a 'clumpy' feel to your T'ai Chi.

Oh yes - don't forget to remove or loosen your wristwatch or bracelet too, as this will also impede Qi and blood flow.

Best Time & Place

'What time of day should I practise my T'ai Chi and where should I do it?'

My simple answer is that any time is good for T'ai Chi practice.

If you are looking for the most ideal and advantageous time however, then at or just after dawn with the sun rising is best. If not, I find the evening is another calming time during the day. Many teachers will say that the effort put into morning practice results in 2-3 times greater benefit than a similar effort in the evening. Be aware though, that as with any exercise, it should not be done on a full stomach - take your breakfast after your T'ai Chi - you will enjoy both so much more. Try also to avoid T'ai Chi in the midday heat or when your body is cold.

Whatever time you choose it is also an advantage if you can be consistent and not random in your choice of time.

Find a level spot ideally with trees or in a garden, particularly if doing Qi Gong (trees and plants release oxygen in the early morning and so this is the time to maximise the effect).

I find a level, fairly firm beach equally rewarding as you can listen to the tranquil in and out sound of the waves and harmonise your breathing to this major force of nature. An added bonus of the beach is that with the volatile sand your balance and stability will improve, and you can see from your footprint how light your foot fall can become.

A firm flat beach is ideal - especially at dawn

Often you will find that the only option will be to practise indoors. This is certainly not a problem - but try to find a quiet calming area, and obviously try to avoid dusty or traffic-fumed areas.

Finally, as with other exercises, it is best not to practise T'ai Chi when you are suffering an acute illness like influenza or an upset stomach. It is much better to wait until you are recovered.

Impromptu T'ai Chi

T'ai Chi practised as a health exercise has the added advantage of convenience. It can be slotted into any break-time wherever you are and requires only a small space with no special clothing or equipment.

> *Exasperated at work; killing time between appointments; out walking in the park or country side; inspecting and enjoying your garden; raining and you're stuck in your house; on your own and feeling lonely?*

Try a little T'ai Chi or Qi Gong and I guarantee that you will feel a little better and ready to tackle what is coming next. You should find that it will invigorate, refresh and relax you.

The side-effects of impromptu T'ai Chi are that you will be benefiting subconsciously from the qualities that it brings: patience, perseverance, tolerance, discipline and confidence. All ideal assets in a modern environment.

If possible, when you are practising your impromptu T'ai Chi form, you should always try to change into a pair of flat-soled lightweight shoes to 'feel' the ground as heavyweight shoes or trainers will impede foot and leg balance.

If you can, loosen any tight clothing such as ties and cuffs - and don't forget to remove or loosen your wristwatch or bracelet, and of course, turn off your mobile phone!

Oh yes - be aware too that if practising in more formal attire, carrying out the enthusiastic high kick that you had been performing so well during last night's class may end up in an embarrassing moment as tight seams split easily.

Can't sleep?

Don't count sheep - many Qi Gongs can be carried out laying down - or just practise your T'ai Chi breathing. Many of us mentally run through the form at normal practice speed. Not only does it help you to remember the form better, but you will usually find that you are asleep before the end!

The T'ai Chi Salute

When you attend your first T'ai Chi session you may see your teacher and other members at the session holding their hands in a Chinese greeting or salute.

This T'ai Chi courtesy was introduced to me by Dr Paul Lam who used it as a general greeting/farewell. In addition to this, I always use it to start and end all our T'ai Chi forms to emphasise what it means to me.

I was told that the salute has three profound and important messages to impart that signifies so much in relationship to T'ai Chi.

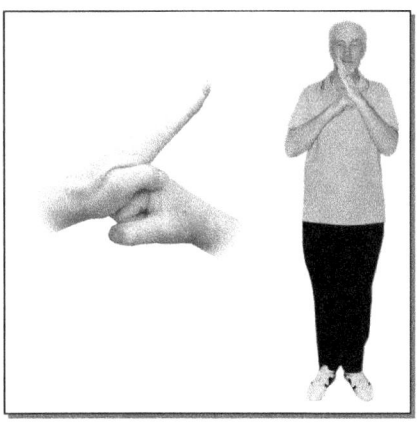

A T'ai Chi Greeting or Salute

The **FIST** formed by the right hand shows that T'ai Chi is powerful. When practised correctly, it is not just a powerful defensive martial art, but also a very effective health defender. Even though the movements appear quiet and relaxed, their practice helps develop a strong and healthy body and an alert and less stressed mind.

The **FOUR STRAIGHT FINGERS** of the left hand are the symbol of friendship. When we learn and practise T'ai Chi together, we are all friends together and all support each other, progressing as one.

The **BENT THUMB** of the left hand is to me the most significant and profound message. This symbolises humility. It reminds us that we all make mistakes and that none of us will ever be perfect – so never worry that you cannot do your forms as well as your friends. Enjoy your T'ai Chi, learning from others around you, and in turn help and encourage each other to achieve the goal.

When combined into the salute, these three elements epitomise the bonding, effective power, enjoyment and well-being that practising T'ai Chi can bring.

Do's & Dont's

Please take a minute to read this list before you move on to start your T'ai Chi practice in earnest.

- **ALWAYS** precede your main T'ai Chi forms with warm up exercises and end with cool-down exercises.
- **DO NOT** force any movements. Move without effort, as though gently swimming in air.
- **NEVER** over exert yourself. If you experience pain or other symptoms, STOP T'ai Chi practice, talk to your teacher and maybe consider consulting your Doctor or Specialist before continuing.
- **AVOID** any abrupt movements. They create tension that will put you off balance and possibly injure muscles.
- **DO NOT** force yourself into a lower stance or bend the knees beyond your comfort zone. Stand up if you feel too much stress on the knees.
- **DO** maintain correct posture. **DO NOT** lean backward or forwards or lock the knees. Keep your back upright so that the spine is balanced on the pelvis, and keep knees aligned over your feet but slightly bent forward (soft).
- **DO** feel free to modify movements that are uncomfortable. Your T'ai Chi should be pleasant and enjoyable, not an endurance contest.
- **DO** wear comfortable loose clothes and shoes that are comfortable and suitable for good balance. For people with diabetes, shoes are especially vital as lack of foot sensitivity is a common problem.
- **DO** seek advice from your teacher if you feel unbalanced or unstable during T'ai Chi. Corrections to your technique or variations to the form will be suggested.
- **DO** remain mentally alert. Be conscious of the movements that you are making.
- **DO** drink water frequently. Hydration is important.
- **DO** enjoy your T'ai Chi.

After Your First Lessons

When we first start T'ai Chi we try to take on board everything that our teacher tells us - usually becoming overwhelmed and often confused. Your teacher corrects the mistakes and posture of you and others, and you listen avidly to everything said.

Then you go home........

'What was I told?'

'I'm confused!'

'I can't remember the sequence or detail of a movement'

'Was I doing it right because I wasn't corrected?'

'I don't think that I am moving the same amount and with the same smoothness as the others.....why didn't my teacher correct me?'

'I remember the teacher talking about being relaxed yet my "droopy" posture was corrected.'

'I chilled so much during Qi Gong that I nearly fell asleep.'

'I concentrated hard on achieving the movements and was then corrected for being tense.......'

Now you begin to worry that T'ai Chi is so complex that you will never be able to learn it. Of course you will.......

Confused, lost? ... You will never be able to remember everything that your teacher tells you and certainly will not be able to spontaneously reproduce the movements and form when you are on your own until you have practised conscientiously for some time. You learn and retain a little more each time you attend a group class or session. That is why your teacher will normally call out movements as you learn. When you are on your own, practise the bits you remember. Nobody is checking on you or examining you. Concentrate on trying to achieve a smoothness and flowing movement. Don't tense up and freeze with 'what do I do next?'.

Poor posture? ... Everyone's posture and movement ability is different, as is the time taken to produce a noticeable improvement. Your teacher will only correct you if your movement is dangerous, or if you are ready for a progressive improvement hint. There is a difference between a droopy or sloppy relaxed posture and the T'ai Chi meaning of relaxed. In this context the body is soft and loose but 'ready to go'. Imagine an elastic band strung between the index finger of each hand. With the hands together the band droops and has no potential. Move the hands apart until the band is just tight - it is now in a relaxed but primed condition. This is the state of softness in T'ai Chi, allowing the potential of controlled further movement. Pulling the hands apart to stretch and tense the band illustrates this, (see more on page 57).

Too relaxed or over-tense? ... As a beginner learning the controlled relaxation of T'ai Chi and Qi Gong, it is to be expected that this new lack of tension may overflow into sleepiness. Again better control will come with practice. Similarly, when you are learning a new T'ai Chi form movement, the concentration required will often cause tension until it is perfected.

Practise .... Think - Ask - Observe .... Practise

So now read on and I will introduce some of the basic precepts and principles of T'ai Chi movement, posture and mental attitude.

CHAPTER 7
INTRODUCING A FEW WORDS YOU'LL MEET

As you start your T'ai Chi journey you will find that your teacher will often use words and terms that are unfamiliar to you to describe actions and to describe posture and movement.

Therefore, before we start to look at posture and movement, I'll explain some of the more common words, phrases and terminology that are used regularly and which will appear in the descriptions that follow. As you progress, a deeper understanding of their meaning should start to become apparent.

Other terms and expressions that you meet that are not listed here will be explained to you as you progress, either by your teacher, or in other more detailed books on T'ai Chi that you find and read.

The Terminology of T'ai Chi

Beginners to T'ai Chi are often confused by the spellings and descriptive terminology used.

Don't worry about it - the Chinese written and spoken language is full of anomalies, pictorial characters and dialect interpretation. The most common effects of this are spelling and literal interpretation. You will also find that different teachers and T'ai Chi styles may use different terms for similar actions.

Before we look at a few basic terms in detail let's consider a few generalities.

'Allegorical' and 'Real' terms

Literal translations of allegorical terms are often used to describe T'ai Chi movements, particularly in documented lists of the sequence of movements. Here the terms are usually compared to an animal stance or everyday action. Again translator licence may produce different terms for the same action, for example:

> Big Bird Spreading its Wings or White Crane Parts its Wings…?
> Leisurely tying the Coat or Lazily Tucking Clothes…?
> Carry Tiger to the Mountain or Embrace Tiger and Push the Mountain…?

Sometimes terms use 'real' terminology where the term is directly descriptive of the action. A few examples of this that you may meet are:

Punch Under Elbow.
Covered Hand Punch.
Low Toe Kick.

Your teacher may also sometimes use his own descriptive terms which may be different to those used by another.

Spelling - Western or Pin Yin?

Peking or Beijing…?
T'ai Chi or Taiji…?
Chi or Qi…?
Chi Kung or Qi Gong…?
Tan Tien or Dan Tien…?

Different spelling but the same meaning! The first example in each case is the 19th century standardised western translation (Wade-Giles). The second is the one advised by the People's Republic of China known as Pin Yin.

Pin Yin is progressively becoming the spelling of choice in martial arts but in reality both spellings are commonly used and you will meet both versions of them (and sometimes others) as you progress.

What do you mean by ....?

Here are explanations of a few common words and phrases that crop up regularly.

Bubbling Well (Yong Quan)

In Chinese medicine and Qi Gong there are many key meridian and acupuncture points. T'ai Chi and Qi Gong will frequently refer to some of these.

One of the first of many that you may meet is the 'Bubbling Well' *(Yong Quan)*. This refers to a point located around the ball of the foot, a significant point in T'ai Chi, used to help build Qi when rooted. It is a major energy entry point and is used to direct energy to and from the ground. Importantly it is a point where of all six of the acupuncture meridians that traverse the legs come together and focus their energy.

It has special relevance in Sun Form where it is used as the platform for the style's characteristic follow through step.

Two other important energy points that you will come across early on are:

The Centre of Vitality *(Ming Men)*: Located in the small of the back and also associated with the basic posture stance. This is mentioned on page 65.

The Palace of Toil *(Lao Gong)*: Located in the palm of the hand where the middle finger touches when making a fist.

Chi (Qi)

Chi (Qi) translates as vital (healing) energy or life force derived from air and breathing, and is integral and central to understanding and practising T'ai Chi. In order to differentiate the term from the alternative translation associated with the name T'ai Chi previously described, I will normally use the 'Qi' spelling in this book when referring to this energy.

You will find a little more information on how and why Qi relates to your T'ai Chi practice on page 19. However, the subject warrants much more coverage than we've given there and I plan that this will form the basis of a future book.

It is essential that the concept of *Qi* is considered by all who practise the art of T'ai Chi, whether in its martial form or as a health exercise. Belief in its power is not essential but a general understanding and appreciation of its concepts and effects are required if you really want to add depth to your T'ai Chi.

Chi Kung (Qi Gong)

In general terms this refers to a gamut of medative movement and breathing exercises. *Qi Gong* normally translates as energy cultivation or breathing exercises. *(Qi is energy or breath. Gong is work, practice, training or skill.)*

This has been explained in more depth earlier on page 21 of this book.

I think it is fair to say that you can practise Qi Gong very effectively and never visit T'ai Chi, but you cannot practise T'ai Chi without understanding the basic principles of Qi Gong. T'ai Chi is a martial art developed from basic Qi Gong movement.

Dan Tien (Tantien)

In Qi Gong this refers to an area in the abdomen centred approximately a three finger measurement both inside the abdomen and below the navel. In simple terms it is considered to be the main central store of Qi energy, and is also the physical centre of gravity of the body. This makes it pivotal in every sense in T'ai Chi movement.

Commonly defined as a ball around the tummy area, in major T'ai Chi practice the Dan Tien is sometimes defined as the whole area between the hip and the arm pit which should be considered as one protective ball *(Iron Shirt)*.

The Dan Tien will be referred to often by your teacher, as even for beginners not familiar with the deeper aspects of energy balance, this part of the body plays a significant role in learning posture and movement.

As you progress to greater depths you will probably learn of other Dan Tien energy centres, a second one in the upper part of the chest and a third in the centre of the forehead.

Eight Energies & Five Steps (13 Postures)

Traditional teaching refers to 'Thirteen Postures' which cover the basic movement aspects of T'ai Chi. These are comprised of eight 'Energies' or 'Gates' which relate to the power *(Jin)* movements, and five 'Steps' which relate to the directions of movement when performing a form.

Whether or not this is discussed with you at an early stage in your T'ai Chi journey will depend upon your teacher and the type of class you are in. A general overview is provided on page 97.

Five Elements

In Chinese philosophy the Five Elements (Water, Wood, Fire, Earth and Metal) are considered to be the basic components of the Universe. Many of the facets of Qi Gong (and hence T'ai Chi) are moulded around these elements which interconnect and have major links with each other.

The relationships between the elements transform themselves into many things. These include the relationship between the body's energy meridians and vital organs, movement description, emotional responses, colours, seasons, times of the day and many other aspects.

Further information can be found on page 94.

Form

A Form can refer to two aspects in T'ai Chi. Its primary definition is the name given to the sequence of movements carried out - as when we refer to *Sun 73 Step Form*, or *Yang 108 Form*, or *Chen Short Form*, or *Chen Old Frame Double Straight Sword Form*.

Confusingly for the beginner, the term Form can also refer to an individual set of sub-movements within the form sequence. For example one of movements common to all forms is *Waving Hands Like a Cloud*. This movement itself breaks down into several sub-movements which are often collectively referred to as *The Form of Waving Hands Like a Cloud*.

Frame

As a specific T'ai Chi style evolved, variants within the styles were created. This could mean a change to the overall stance or the speed of practice, or even the creation of a new practice sequence. To categorise these the term 'Frame' is generally used.

Common examples that you may meet are:

Large or Short Frame: This refers to the overall stance - large is a wide and low posture (legs apart, arms open); short is a narrow and upright posture (legs close together arms closer to the body).

Fast or Slow Frame: This refers to the movement speed of the practice or application.

Old or New Frame: This refers to cases where the original traditional (old) sequence has been superseded by a new sequence that maintains all the disciplines of the original. (This normally applies to changes made in early years and not to the several modern shorter and competition forms created by the Chinese Committees over the last 60 years.)

Jin Energy

Just as *Qi (Chi)* is defined as the internal energy that 'feeds' T'ai Chi, then *Jin* refers to the external energy - the physical force - that the movements of T'ai Chi generate. It is a subject that is essential to understand when pursuing the martial aspect of T'ai Chi, and just like Qi deserves more than the simple reference given to it in this book for beginners.

Jin energy is moved around the body (theoretically in a spiral fashion) to be used internally just to power muscles, etc., or it can be used to provide external power such as in a punch or push. The categories of the types of application of external power are called the Eight Energies. These are listed with a simple explanation on page 97. Control of this power, both in destination and quantity is the essence of all T'ai Chi actions.

- **Fa Jin** This refers to explosive or expulsive energy, where the movement dynamics are speeded up, projecting the force with added acceleration to greatly increase its impact. *'Fa' means to issue or release.*

Note:

A very simplistic explanation that I use to explain T'ai Chi energy to beginners is to consider a car battery:

Qi provides the charge for the battery; Jin is the power from the battery that works the starter, lights, radio, etc. To start the car requires Fa Jin - a large amount of battery power applied as a surge to turn the engine. (I'm sure we've all experienced the effect of a flat battery at some time or other!) Another example of uncontrolled Fa Jin would be the explosive effect of accidentally short-circuiting the battery terminals - not advised!

Kua

You will find that your teacher may refer to *Kua* when talking about leg movement.

A common misconception is that Kua is the waist. This is incorrect. Basically Kua refers to the movement of the hip joints (which in turn will move the waist). Fundamentally Kua is responsible for the integration of the upper and lower body. Kua plays a fundamental part in all turning and movement from one side of the body to the other. It is the pivot point for the upper torso. The better you are at using the Kua, the better your body will be safely coordinated when making turns or looking over your shoulder.

As you progress with your T'ai Chi, your teacher should start to expand the concept of the hip action or Kua. A simple explanation of the essence of Kua movement is can be found on page 81.

Push(ing) or Sticky Hands

Traditional martial T'ai Chi training covers two basic aspects, *Form* - body movement practice, and *Application* - the use of these practised movements to provide the intended purpose against an opponent.

Pushing Hands is an initial set of 'partner' work designed to enable each person to interact and experiment to test the effectiveness of each others awareness and movement, and to instil the discipline of control. The objective is for partners to work together to teach each other. It is not an exercise to try to dominate each other.

Repeating cyclically and in the same order, one partner starts to apply gently force to the other who will at first yield then resist by applying a counter force, at which point the original 'aggressor' will yield and the receiving partner take on the role of pushing. The pusher's force is varied and this develops the skill of detecting and matching the force by the person receiving.

With its pushing and yielding, receiving and giving techniques, pushing hands teaches the skills - equally applicable to general life as in a martial world - of remaining grounded and holding position, matching like with like (verbally and mentally as well as physically) and not giving in to the excesses of anger or fear, aggression or timidity.

Your teacher may introduce you to a basic pushing hands routine in order to help to remove the excess of exaggerated movement that most enthusiastic beginners will experience, and to help improve posture control and awareness of energy transfer.

Silk Reeling and Spiralling Energy

Silk Reeling is often used as a general term that is applied to flowing T'ai Chi movement. It is also applied to a series of advanced Qi Gong exercises designed to promote awareness and control of using 'Spiralling Energy' to promote power and flexible response to movements, *Chan Si Jin(g)*. The allegorical term Silk Reeling relates to the spiralling movements of a silk-worm larva as it forms its cocoon, and the actions required later to unravel it and draw an unbroken thread that we can use to make fabric.

'Spiralling Energy' an advanced concept, not normally explained to or understood by the novice, but one that it is essential to develop (guided by a teacher) if you are aspiring to understand T'ai Chi practice to a greater depth.

An introduction Silk Reeling and Spiral Energy can be found on page 92, but your teacher will be best able to judge when to introduce the concept to you.

Six Harmonies

This term refers to the three internal and three external body harmonies which summarise a correct and effective T'ai Chi movement. This is explained further on page 89.

The internal harmonies refer to mental and energy states, and the external harmonies refer to correctly aligned and balanced body posture. A simple understanding of their relationship (harmony) is fundamental in starting to gain an understanding of T'ai Chi and gaining deeper benefit from it.

Song (Sung)

The Chinese term *Song or Sung* means relaxed - don't confuse it with the western term for vocal harmony and expression. In a T'ai Chi context 'relaxed' too does not have the same meaning as the western definition of being free from tension, loose, laid back, all of which imply a sloppy or limp posture.

In T'ai Chi 'relaxed' *Song* is defined as a controlled state of awareness and alertness - ready to respond but not tensed. There is more about *Song* on page 57.

Style

A T'ai Chi Style normally refers to the series of movements created by a specific Master. Typical Styles are Chen, Yang, Wu, Sun, Lee (see "A Potted History of T'ai Chi" on page 149).*In this respect styles can be considered analogous to dance styles such as Waltz, Tango, etc.*

Styles can also have sub-styles such as derivatives *Chen Old Frame* and *Chen New Frame*, or the Yang derivative *Cheng Man Ching Yang Style*, etc.

T'ai Chi (Taiji)

Taken literally *T'ai (Tai)* approximately translates as grand, big, etc.

Unfortunately a confusion arises with the word *Chi(Ji)*. In our own language we are aware that there are several words that can have different meanings yet share the same spelling (examples include words such as *flat*, *book*, *kind*, etc.). Chinese translation is no different and the word pronounced *Chi(Ji)* is an example.

The word 'Chi' is normally associated with energy and the control of it in our practice, as in 'Chi Kung' with a Pin Yin spelling *Qi*. However in the case of the term 'T'ai Chi' the Pin Yin is *Ji* not *Qi*, with a translation of 'Ultimate'. This gives us the definition of T'ai Chi as 'Grand or Supreme Ultimate'.

Ultimate what? The 'Ultimate' is the movement and the application of powerful energy or force, but we need a little more to qualify it.

- **T'ai Chi Chuan***(Taiji Quan)* is the most common term used and refers to the (empty) hand form of T'ai Chi with the word *Chuan (Quan)* meaning a fist. This provides the literal translation of hand form as 'Grand or Supreme Ultimate Fist or Boxing'.

In the modern world, especially in a non-martial context, the use of the term 'T'ai Chi Chuan' to describe the hand form has tended to be reduced back to the generalisation 'T'ai Chi' - in fact this shorter term now usually implies any variant of the art. As you progress however you will learn that the practice of T'ai Chi can be carried out not only with empty hands, but also with the addition of a weapon or similar item which extends the range of movement and balance. Additional words are therefore added the term T'ai Chi to signify this. Examples that you may hear are:

- **T'ai Chi Chien** *(Taiji Jian)* refers to the sword forms of T'ai Chi, the word *Chien (Jian)* meaning a straight double-edged sword.

- **T'ai Chi Dow** *(Taiji Tao)* refers to the sabre or broadsword forms of T'ai Chi, the word *Dao (Tao)* referring to a slashing type weapon.

- **T'ai Chi Shan** *(Taiji Shan)* refers to the fan form of T'ai Chi, the word *Shan* meaning fan.

- **T'ai Chi Gun, T'ai Chi Chiang** *(Taiji Gun, Taiji Qiang)* refer to the staff and spear form of T'ai Chi, the word *Gun* meaning staff and *Chiang (Qiang)* meaning spear.

Wuji, Wu Chi (Posture of Infinity)

When you start any T'ai Chi form or Qi Gong, your teacher may refer to the Wuji Posture. This is the classic 'relaxed' T'ai Chi starting posture that we adopt when commencing Qi Gong or a T'ai Chi form, or if taking a break between movements.

It is a focusing stance that loosens and aligns the body prior to commencing our practice. Described in Taoist terms as the 'posture of infinity', where we can reflect and contemplate our bodies, it symbolically represents the 'great emptiness' of the original universal void.

A description of this very important posture is provided on page 65.

Yin & Yang

When ever you see reference to T'ai Chi you see the Yin & Yang symbol. *Don't get the term 'Yang' used in this sense confused with the name of a style of T'ai Chi created by Yang Lu-Ch'an.*

This circular symbol, with its two expanding complementary parts, each which retain a little of each other, combined with the serpentine flowing nature of their moulding together, can be considered to be representative of T'ai Chi. It defines the balanced relationship of T'ai Chi practice, and also the flowing, serpentine style of the movement.

As T'ai Chi skills develop so will the appreciation of how this symbol relates to its practice and philosophy in so many ways.

We will revisit "Yin & Yang" on page 87 and consider some of the fundamental, easy-to-understand concepts so that you will start to see how you can use the symbol to relate to and improve your practice.

> Note:
>
> *In addition to the literal meaning of the three previous terms above, there are also many other associations and deeper allegorical meanings for them that you may discover. For example you may meet the following description, buried within the depths of Chinese philosophy and associated with the 2000 year old classic 'Book of Changes' I Ching, paraphrased thus:*
>
> *'T'ai Chi came from Wu Chi or the mental state of nothingness. When started into motion, the Wu Chi creates T'ai Chi which becomes the mother of Yin and Yang'.*
>
> *Lost? I thought you might be..... Don't worry about it. This sort of philosophic detail is not intended for or needed by the beginner. Simply think of Wu Chi as a static, focussing posture stimulating the build up of energy; T'ai Chi as the movement and the explosion of practice; Yin and Yang as the harmony and control of the movements.*

Zhan Zhuang (Standing Like a Tree)

The accepted translation of Zhan Zhuang *(pronounced Jan Jong)* is 'Standing Like a Tree'. Zhan Zhuang is one of the few major Qi Gong or exercise routines that involves no direct physical movement, yet combines all the elements of an ideal whole body exercise: the physical development of health, strength, muscle tone and posture control combined with internal calmness, philosophy and personality enhancement.

As such it is used extensively in Chinese medical therapy in hospitals and clinics for the treatment of a wide range of conditions, and also by serious students of many internal martial arts (not only T'ai Chi), where it is used to develop full physical and mental body control. Research in modern China into its effects has endorsed its benefits. Originally a martial arts 'secret', it is now practised by increasing numbers of people throughout China and is part of the training of some of the country's top athletes to provide increased blood circulation, greater breath capacity and enhanced muscle tone.

Its best though that you learn basic Zhan Zhuang with a teacher and that you don't start to practise it until you have learnt the basic concepts of posture and simple form. A general introduction to this exercise is provided in Chapter 13 .

Chapter 8
Getting Started

In this section I will introduce some of the basic precepts and principles of movement, posture and mental attitude. Hopefully this will provide an initial grounding for you as a beginner, and answer more of your questions.

Don't worry about the detail of these concepts. The simplified descriptions in this book are intended to help reduce your trepidation and assist you to enjoy the learning experience and crave more. As you gather more information from books, your teacher and from practice, you will gradually appreciate them in more depth.

The Rooted Tree

Just like a tree, T'ai Chi gains its strength from its rooted stance. Relaxed movement promotes the transfer of body weight to the legs. The more you can relax, the greater the weight that sinks down to your legs.

A straight posture permits the flow of Qi (energy) and helps focus body weight onto a small area. A perfect combination of relaxation and a completely straight posture is difficult to attain, particularly for beginners, and can lead to a little leg or back pain which then causes involuntarily tension and incorrect posture as the load on the legs is relieved. These effects will reduce the value of the exercise and for some will lead to abandoning T'ai Chi altogether.

If you are a beginner don't worry. Only a lucky few of you will achieve anything like perfect posture immediately - it has to be developed within the constraints of your age and health. As long as you try to ensure that you have no tension in the back of the knees, practice will progressively increase ability.

So why does T'ai Chi put more load on your legs which are normally carrying our body weight anyway?

Try this experiment:

> Stand upright as you would normally around the home.
> Feel the weight of the body on the hips and knees.
> Now soften the knees.
> Feel the body weight shift to the leg muscles relieving pressure on the joints.

By relaxing the knee joints T'ai Chi takes body weight that is mostly supported by the body's bony skeleton (which causes joint wear and potential replacement as we age), and transfers the support to the muscles of the leg and straightens the spine. No longer is body movement comparable to driving a car with no suspension - the suspension springs are activated!

This continued exposure to an increased load develops the leg muscles, particularly the thigh muscles. This increased leg strength not only gives explosive strength in martial T'ai Chi, but also provides the ability to release the coiled spring of energy and move very fast when required.

However, as with any serious art, in order to acquire such proficiency, a great deal of patience and dedication is required to aspire to the ultimate level. Many, although practising regularly, either from ignorance or laziness, do not follow the basic precepts so meticulously, and they inevitably adopt incorrect postures or tense up. Unfortunately correction cannot be achieved immediately. It has to be progressive - a little gradual correction at each session.

Very importantly, when we are practising T'ai Chi for health, stance does not need to reach anywhere near the extremes of the martial artist. Many that I teach start seated and then may only improve to what visually appears as a 'shuffle' T'ai Chi - but consider the reality of what they have actually achieved in added mobility, confidence and balance.

It is very important and a sign of a good teacher, that beginners should reach a level of stability within their own comfort zone, with movement and posture relaxed and not damaging.

Basic Posture

Now finally we'll get around to start talking about basic posture and how it's application makes T'ai Chi a complete holistic exercise.

What did my teacher tell me when he corrected my posture?
How should I stand?
How do I breathe?
Should I close my eyes?

These are some of the questions a beginner asks. Before we consider the way to achieve fluid movement, let's consider how the individual parts of the body should be treated to safely maximise T'ai Chi benefit. The information provided here is not intended to replace your teacher, but hopefully it will help and remind you what your teacher told you.

General Body Posture

Repeating again the message that has been written so many times already, when practising T'ai Chi you must let your body remain relaxed (this term is explained next) and natural at all times, without unnecessary tension. Be aware though that relaxation does not mean being droopy or sloppy as if you were a dead weight.

The body and head should be upright, as if suspended centrally from a piece of string. Loosen your joints and allow the body to assume a natural position without creating artificial stances or trying too much.

Basic Stance

Remember that T'ai Chi is gentle and therapeutic, providing balanced exercise to all parts of the body. A key maxim is that the body will gain its strength and stability as a tree does through the trunk and roots, in our case the legs and carefully placed feet. The upper half of the body will be flexible and yielding, yet strong, as are the branches of a tree. When we perform our T'ai Chi we coordinate upper and lower body movement.

Even if seated all these principles will still apply. Those that have severely limited movement can imagine the movement and still get benefit from effective stimulation.

A Relaxed Posture

As mentioned earlier, when you are practising T'ai Chi we talk about the body being 'relaxed'. In a T'ai Chi context this does not have the same meaning as the western definition of being free from tension, loose or laid back. This can imply a sloppy or limp posture. In T'ai Chi we define 'relaxed' more as a controlled state of awareness and alertness. The Chinese term that we use for this is *'Sung* or *Song'* (not the same word as our definition which refers to vocal harmony and expression).

Let me try to illustrate this with a simple analogy to a rubber band.

When the band is held loosely it is slack and has no power. It is relaxed in the accepted western way - but it is sloppy and loose.

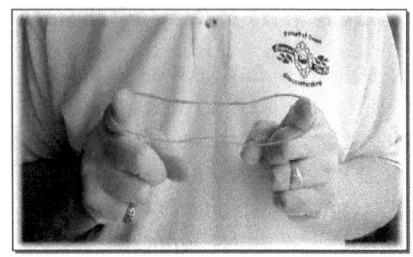

If the band is held taught (bought to a minimum tension), it is 'primed', and holds a dormant energy. This state exemplifies T'ai Chi's definition of 'relaxed' - a state of focused readiness, aware of latent *qi* energy - and one that we should try to maintain throughout our practice. All our muscles and tendons are gently 'primed'. The body can react instantly, but is not in a state of unnecessary tension, expending and wasting energy and causing stress. Think of a car engine smoothly ticking over waiting for the traffic lights to change.

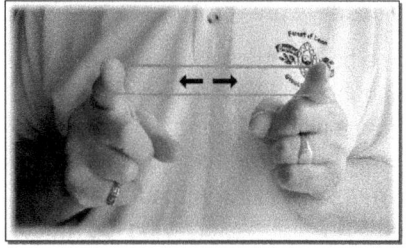

This is the state of 'Relaxation' that we should always try to achieve when practising our T'ai Chi.

When the band is stretched the energy is amplified and stored in the Dan Tien *(yin movement, qi energy)*. As soon as the band is released back the acquired energy is utilised, *(yang movement, jin energy)*, and the band returns back to its minimum tension state, but is not slack or loose.

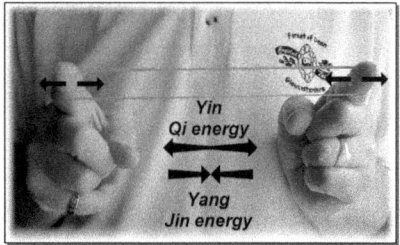

The Head and Neck

Keep your head upright at all times without creating any tension. Align your head and neck with your spine. Imagine your head is suspended by a piece of string, but resist the temptation to stretch it upward as if light headed or floating.

Ensure that the neck allows the head to easily rotate from side to side. Do not, however, lean your head in any direction: don't look down and definitely don't extend the head backward by looking up and over. (This can potentially cause a stress fracture, especially in those with osteoporosis.)

The Chest and Back

Once correct breathing is mastered, the chest and back posture will invariably be correct. However, for beginners it is very important that poor back and chest posture do not generate pain.

Assuming that the basic leg stance with soft knees is in place, the upper back should be raised to allow the chest to hollow. A hollow chest will minimise tension and encourage a natural breathing rhythm.

Never lean forward, backward or sideways. Not only will this cause lower back pain, it also contradicts the T'ai Chi concept of a rooted, balanced stance. If you are leaning, your body is unstable, and from a martial concept, leaves you vulnerable to a pull or push from an opponent which will completely topple you.

The Legs

Whatever you are doing day or night the chances are that you are using your legs to some degree to support the weight of your body. Even when you are lying down you will use leg muscles to turn your body. In T'ai Chi the legs are definitely an essential factor in your practice.

Depending upon the style of T'ai Chi that you are learning (Sun, Yang, Chen, etc.), the static leg stance will differ. Some styles of T'ai Chi have lower, quite wide stances, with body weight supported between the two legs and both knees bent to give a wide, low posture. Other styles such as Sun have a much more upright stance with a follow-through "nimble" half step on many movements, dynamically altering weight distribution for each new position.

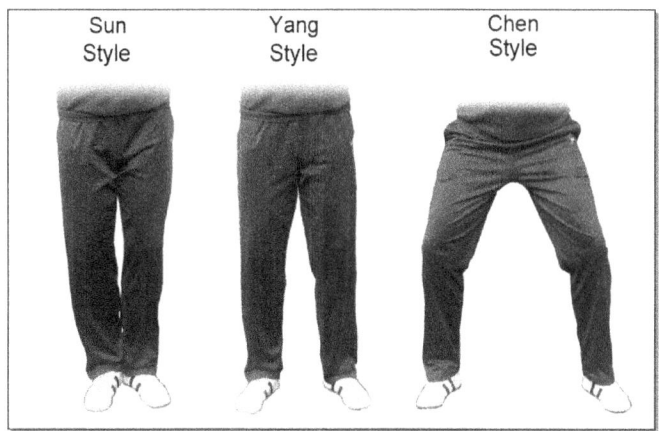

Typical Leg Stance Positions

The Feet

The feet are one of the key elements in T'ai Chi's static and moving stances. They form the root to the ground and as such at least one foot is securely weight bearing and firmly flat on the floor. (Except of course if making advanced jumps and skip steps where both may leave the floor momentarily.)

As a general rule when forward movement such as a single step or walk is required, stability is first ascertained by rooting one leg. Only then is the stepping foot moved forward, with the heel placed on the floor first, then the ball of the foot, and finally the toes, just as if you were walking on slippery rocks or ice. This ensures that the movement can easily be aborted without loosing stability.

Place ..... Feel (is the position safe?) **...... Transfer** (weight)

Similarly, when stepping backwards (a retreat step), stability through one leg is established first. This time it is the toe followed by the ball of the stepping foot that is placed on the floor first, then the heel lowered down as the weight is transferred.

This controlled light movement (heel to toe, toe to heel) is carried out when stepping forward, backward or at an angle. This method of movement (which we have all used when walking on an unstable surface) provides maximum stability and is one of the reasons that T'ai Chi improves balance and confidence in the less able.

Stepping is explored in more detail on page 70.

The Knees

The knee is a very complex and potentially delicate hinge joint. Whenever your step movement calls for you adopt a forward bow stance, it is very important that the knee should be moved forward towards the toes but never allowed to project beyond the end of them. This would cause enormous stress on the joint as the body weight starts to project forward and not downwards to the foot.

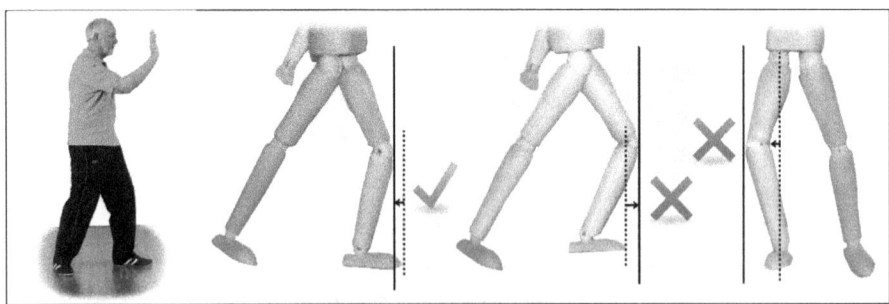

Safe Knee Movement

Another common cause of knee damage to be aware of and avoid, is twisting the knee sideways out of its alignment with the hip and ankle during weight shift.

There is further discussion on the knee position later in the description of Kua on page 81.

Always monitor your leg and foot movement to ensure that you don't fall into bad habits.

The Shoulders and Arms

The shoulders should be relaxed, rounded and level which each other at all times. Do not lift one shoulder above the other as this creates shoulder and neck tension. This is especially true when rotating the arms, which should never raise the shoulder joint. As the shoulder joint rotates you should feel the ball of the shoulder joint turning smoothly in its socket.

Basic Shoulder Movement

Arms should always be slightly bent, relaxed and never locked at the elbow joint. The elbows themselves, and to a lesser extent the wrists, apart from a few exceptions, should generally form a shallow angle even when the hands and forearms are raised above head height. When at your side, arms should be held loosely away from the body. *Imagine there is a birds egg held under your armpit - too tight and it will break, too loose and it will fall.*

The Hands

The hands movements are very significant because of the intricate movements and patterns they have to execute, often with a spiralling type movement. As you will discover if you move to more advanced levels of T'ai Chi, there is a lot more depth to hand movement than is described here.

When the palm is open the fingers should be open. In effect this means extended slightly apart from each other in a natural way, not splayed wide and not pressing tightly against one another. This will maximise Qi flow which will usually be felt as a tingling sensation in the finger tips. The gap between the thumb and the index finger should be a little wider, as from a martial aspect you may need to grab. *(Imagine you need to reach out to grab a round bar.)*

One significant point to mention is the fist. The fingers should be closed into the palm but should remain fairly loose not clenched tight. The thumb is bent loosely over the nail of the index finger to sit on top of the middle finger. In T'ai Chi we never enclose the thumb with the fingers. Conversely, many Qi Gongs do have the thumb enclosed by the fingers, specifically to apply pressure to key meridian points that are located on the palm.

With punching arm movements the knuckles may end vertical or horizontal. However, make any necessary wrist twist at the start of the movement not the end so that the knuckle position is stable before the delivery arm extension.

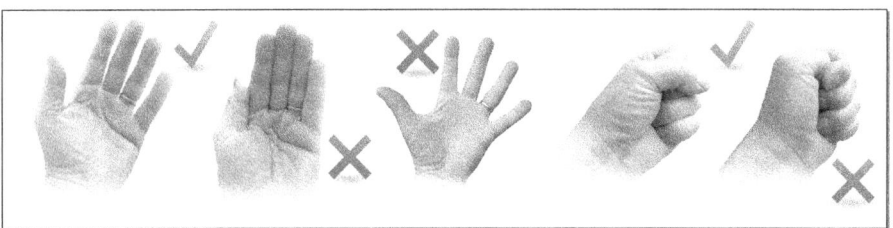

Basic Hand Posture

The Mouth

The mouth plays an important part in the breathing process. Ideally breathing should be through the nose and so the lips should be closed. If possible try to develop the habit of keeping the tip of the tongue touching the roof of the mouth as this helps breathing and is also an aid to keeping the mouth moist.

The Eyes

The eyes are important as they feed back external information to the body. Although it is acceptable to close them during Qi Gong, you should not do so during T'ai Chi form as they are a key factor in posture and balance control.

In common with other major parts of the body the eyes should be relaxed - but not closed. They should generally be focused forward into the middle distance. When you have to make a movement to a side direction, the head should move first, allowing the eyes to establish the extent and direction of the movement a fraction before the rest of the body movement.

When stepping backward it is essential that the eyes look forward. Trying to look obliquely behind causes disorientation and results in poor balance control - a major factor in falls. We don't have eyes in the back of our head so looking forward at least keeps the correct orientation plane for the brain to relate to.

In our falls prevention sessions we always teach that you should glance behind FIRST to see if there are any obstacles, then look forward again BEFORE stepping back.

Chapter 9
How To Achieve Posture & Movement

Now that we have established how the body's major parts and limbs should be used when practising T'ai Chi, let's consider how weight shift through the legs should interact to achieve simple, fluid movement.

Positions and movements are compared here in both Yang and Sun Style so that if you wish you can experience the different characteristics of both styles. A small reference may also be made to the martial purpose of the movements, as by visualising the movement, your intent and posture will be more likely to be correct.

The selection here illustrates key movements and are described with the beginner in mind. There are many more movements than these, but you will progressively learn more as you are taught your specific style and form.

The Basic Starting Posture

When Standing

The first thing is to ensure that the initial position that you adopt before any T'ai Chi or Qi Gong practice, seated or standing, consists of a loose relaxed upright posture. This is an essential preparation to enable you to focus correctly and 'charge' the Dan Tien. Usually when you are comfortable in this position, you will find that the tips of your fingers will tingle as blood and Qi circulate freely. This stance is referred to as 'The Posture of Infinity - Wuji (Wu Chi)', and allegorically represents the "great emptiness" of the original universe.

Wuji provides posture awareness, loosening the body and correctly aligning the spine. As well as being used as a starting posture it may also be used as a break between movements. The leg stance varies with T'ai Chi style, but in this book we will only consider the Qi Gong, Yang and Sun style.

66 *Simplifying T'ai Chi*

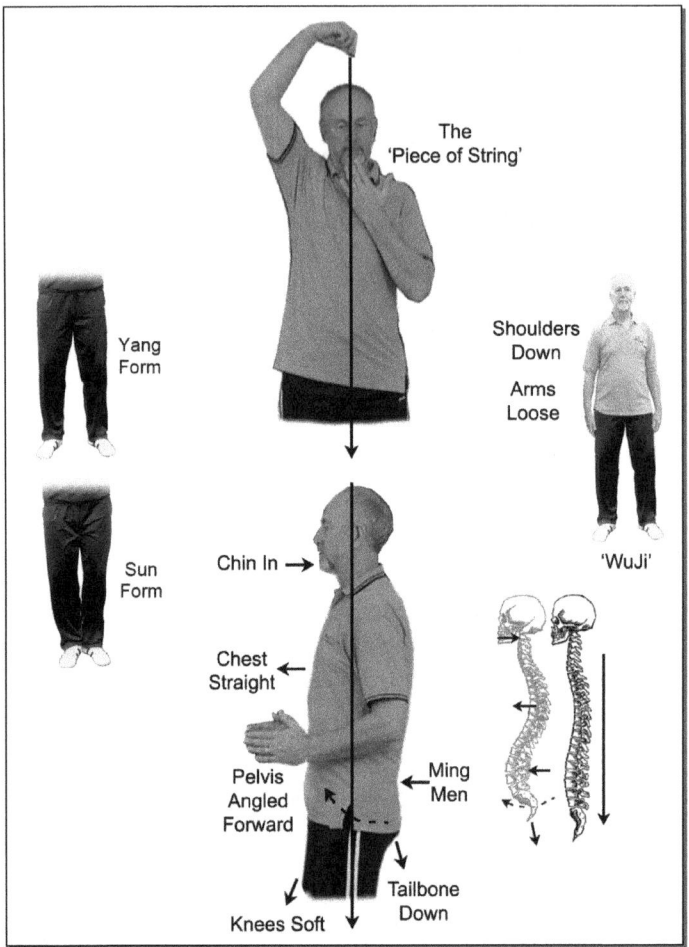

Starting Posture - Achieving Wuji

- Distribute your body weight equally on both feet with the soles flat on the ground. In most styles, including Yang, or for Qi Gong, stand with the feet apart and angle the toes out a little. In Sun style the feet are placed closer together with heels almost touching, again with toes angled out.

- Remove the tension from behind the knees so they soften and bend just slightly forward with the body weight supported by the leg muscles. Ensure that the kneecaps align with the angled toes.

- Hold your head erect and look straight ahead with your chin tucked comfortably in. Imagine that you are suspended centrally by a piece of string.

- Now to straighten your spine. After a little practising you will find that this is achieved by rolling your pelvis forward to tip it slightly, lowering your tail-bone *(coccyx)*. This position is similar to sitting on the edge of a fence or high stool, and causes a point between the 2nd & 3rd lumber vertebrae, *Ming Men*, to move towards the front.

The spine will now be relatively straight and not curving as in a normal 'western' posture.

Stop and check that your head is not leaning forward or backwards. If it is, you will find the weight on your soles of your feet biased towards the toes or heel.

- Ensure there is no tension in your neck. Relax your shoulders pulling them slightly down and rotate them fractionally outward so they become gently rounded.

- Allow arms to hang loosely by your sides and hold them slightly away from the body with a slight 'soft' bend at the elbows. Imagine there is a birds egg held under your armpit - too tight and it will break, too loose and it will fall.

- You will then be ready to start your T'ai Chi form or Qi Gong. If you are just focussing you mind, then it is customary to bring your hands to the front of your tummy, rotating your wrists so that backs of hands face forward, with the palms facing the Dan Tien.

Check that all parts of your body are relaxed, paying particular attention to the neck, the chest and the stomach and lower back.

Once this posture is achieved you should feel as if you are gently suspended by a piece of string attached to the top of your head and your body should feel loose but have controlled stability. Spend a moment to ensure that you are maintaining this posture before proceeding with any movements.

Very few beginners find this starting posture comfortable or easy. Persevere, I've taught it to hundreds of people and I can assure you that it will get easier. The reality is that the posture is very demanding on muscles that we may not use as often as we should.

Angling the knees will push the head of the femur inwards, causing the muscles in your buttocks to squeeze. Tilting the pelvis causes the muscles in the stomach area to arch the lumber joints forward and curve the chest inwards, which is balanced by the tucking in of the chin to push the head back and straighten the cervical spine. When the legs are softened with the knees forward not locked, the quads are bought into use and the legs may start to feel tired.

Initially use regular breathing but after a little practice you'll start to experience a natural a lowering feeling, where weight naturally redistributes itself from the upper part of the body down to the lower part. At this point you can start to try diaphragmatic breathing, especially when practising Qi Gong - but don't try too hard, it will happen soon enough. Diaphragmatic breathing is described on page 85.

When Seated

Qi Gong and T'ai Chi for health can be just as beneficial when seated, particularly for the older and less able for whom standing Qi Gong or leg-based movement is not practical.

- Choose a suitable firm supportive chair that is of sufficient height to allow you to sit up with your knees forming a right angle.
- Sit with feet slightly apart with the toes angled out a little. Distribute your body weight equally on both buttocks and if possible ensure the soles of the feet are flat on the ground.
- Remove the tension from behind the knees and try to feel the body weight supported by the buttocks and transferring through the legs to the soles of the feet.
- Try to keep your spine straight, pulling tail-bone *(coccyx)* upward and inward towards the front.
- Without creating tension in your neck, hold your head erect and look straight ahead with your chin tucked comfortably in.
- Ensure there is no tension in your neck. Relax your shoulders pulling them slightly down and rotate them outward so they become gently rounded.
- Place your hands on the top of your thighs, either loosely open or shaped into a loose fist with the thumbs on top.
- After initially settling in this position, it is customary to bring your hands to the front of your tummy, rotating your wrists so that the backs of the hands face forward, with the palms facing the Dan Tien.

Check that all parts of your body are relaxed, paying particular attention to the neck, the chest and the stomach and lower back.

As with the standing position you should feel as if you are gently suspended by a piece of string attached to the top of your head and the body should feel loose but have controlled stability. Spend a moment to ensure that you are maintaining this posture before proceeding with any movements.

Weight Shift

The fundamentals of safe T'ai Chi leg movements require that you understand and can carry out balanced weight shift. The basic principles of this should be practised from the beginning. Your teacher will expand more and develop specific movements when you start to learn form. However, practising the stances here will provide a background and help you to progress a little better with your lessons.

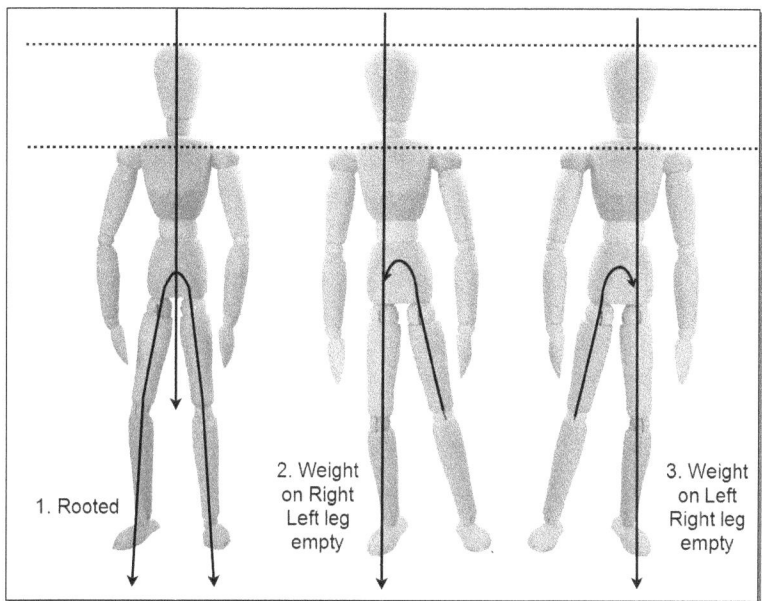

Simple Weight Shift

The following descriptions refer to the picture above:

Basic Rooted Stance (picture inset 1)

This is a T'ai Chi stance where the weight is distributed evenly on both feet. Examples include the basic standing stance described on page 65, and the start stance for most forms and Qi Gong, commonly referred to as the *Horse Stance*.

In most styles of T'ai Chi and Qi Gong the feet point at an outward angle with legs slightly apart when in the basic stance *(picture on page 59.* The knees soften and point over the toes. The upper body aligns downward as if suspended by a piece of string with the pelvis slightly forward as if you are partially sitting on a fence or high stool.

In the Yang Horse Stance the knees soften more and the feet are further apart - as if you are riding a horse. It is essential however, that the knees remain in line over the feet so that the wider that the legs are apart, the lower the body will get. *(Imagine a large box between your feet and knees keeping both of the lower legs vertical.)*

In Sun style the feet are placed closer together with heels almost touching making the overall stance higher. You must still remember to keep the feet at an angle though (toes pointing outwards slightly), to allow the legs to soften as you shift weight, whilst still retaining correct knee/foot/toe alignment.

Weight Shift to Right - Left foot empty *(picture inset 2)*

Here weight is shifted smoothly from the fully rooted position to one side in order to support the body and maintain stability while freeing the leg on the other side to make a movement, e.g. a step, a turn, a kick, etc. In order to maintain stability, it is important that the body remains stable and upright without any leaning to the left or right whilst the movement is completed. The leg that is free is referred to as 'empty'.

To achieve this, the weight bearing leg in the picture *(the right)* sinks a little lower by softening the knee, and the weight is slowly transferred by an internal 'rolling' action across and around the Dan Tien from the left leg which will straighten slightly at the knee. This gives a progressive and controlled weight shift which can be stopped or reversed at any point to adapt to a situation. The movement is smooth and not a jerked, irreversible movement.

The back is kept straight and the shoulders and head remain level. You will also notice that there will be a slight rotation of the hips as the weight transfers. This is essentially 'Sinking the Kua' which is explained in more detail later on page 81.

Weight Shift to Left - Right foot empty *(picture inset 3)*

Weight shift from the right to left is a mirror of the shift described above, moving weight smoothly via the Dan Tien from one leg to the other by fractionally softening the left knee and lengthening the right.

Stepping Forward & Backward

Having mastered static weight shift we can consider a basic stepping sequence.

Stepping should be compared to the procedure that you would adopt when walking on ice or on slippery rocks, i.e. make sure you are stable in the position that you are currently in, then 'test' further onward stability by 'feeling' with the moving foot for a stable stepping area, and only then committing to complete the actual movement. Never place one foot directly in front of the other as if on a tightrope.

Stepping varies with T'ai Chi style. In this book we will only consider the differences between Yang and Sun style.

For beginners the basic Yang stepping stance requires that the heels are typically positioned at least 300mm (12") behind each other with a 150mm (6") sideways spacing, toes angled outwards (knees aligned to toes). Due to its more upright stance Sun requires that the feet are spaced more as in conventional walking with a reduced heel sideways spacing of 50mm (2") and a narrower toe-out angle. The toes of the 'follow-through' step should be near the heel of the front foot.

Chapter 9 How To Achieve Posture & Movement   71

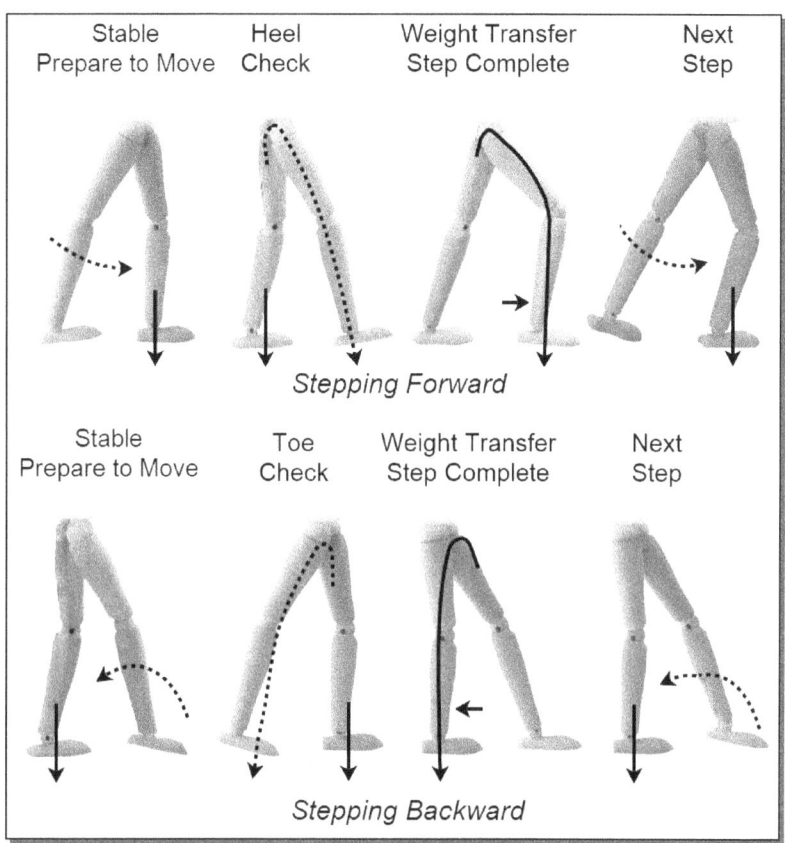

Principles of Stepping Forward and Backward

Stepping Forward

Yang Style: To move forward in Yang style first sink the weight to the static leg. Peel the heel on the now 'empty' stepping leg and step to place the heel on to the ground in front of you. As you step, slightly curve the leg in towards the weight-bearing leg then back out again.

Note: Never place one foot directly in front of the other as if on a tightrope.

Forward Step (Yang)

Once the step distance is set by placing the heel, transfer the weight to the forward leg, rolling smoothly via the Dan Tien. As the weight transfers, the ball of the foot rolls down, lowering the toes to place the foot fully on the floor (1) and forming a simple 'bow stance' with the weight distributed approximately 60% to the bowed leg and 40% to the rear leg. (A description of the bow stance and knee position is discussed later on page 74.) You are then ready to carry out the next movement of the form, or take further steps by continuing the forward weight transfer by repeating the sequence for the other leg (2).

Sun Style: In Sun style the initial placing of the forward foot is straight ahead, similar to conventional walking but still maintaining a slight foot spacing with toes at a slight angle. The heel is placed down first.

Note: Because the Sun Style has a more upright stance, the step distance is shorter than in Yang style.

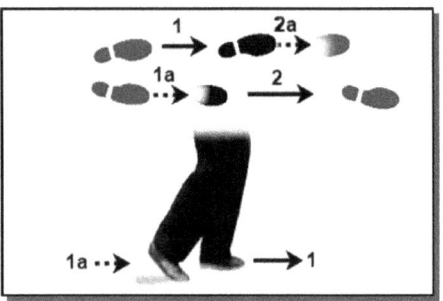

Forward Step (Sun)

Once the distance is set by placing the heel, the weight is transferred to the forward leg smoothly via the Dan Tien, rolling the ball of the foot to lower the toes and root the foot fully on the floor (1). The rear leg stays in alignment with the hips, but follows through with a small step (DON'T just lift the heel up) maintaining an upright stance with the ball of the foot (NOT just the toes) braced slightly to the floor and heel raised slightly. The main centre of gravity is over the forward leg with a small (20-30%) of weight on the ball of the rear foot (1a).

You are then ready to carry out a new movement, or continue making further steps by continuing the forward weight transfer and stepping again (2 & 2a).

All Styles: The back should be kept straight with the pelvis still sitting on the imaginary fence or high stool. The head should be upright and the eyes should remain looking forward and not down at the feet. The knee moves over the toes and never out to the side (as discussed on page 60). Try not to allow the head to bob up and down.

To obtain a bigger step whilst maintaining an upright stance and without leaning forward, you will soon realise that you will have to sink the supporting knee lower allowing the stepping ('free') leg to extend further - but beginners should stay within their comfort zone and keep their stepping distance to a sensible gap.

Moving Backward

Yang Style: To move backward in Yang style sink the weight to the static leg, peeling the heel of the stepping leg off the floor. When stable, lift the now 'empty' stepping leg and place the ball of the foot down on the ground behind you. As you step, slightly curve the leg travel inwards towards the weight-bearing leg then back out again as it moves behind.

Note: Never place one foot directly behind the other as if on a tightrope.

Once the step distance is set by placing the foot behind, transfer the weight to the rear leg smoothly via the Dan Tien, rolling the heel downwards to place the foot fully on the floor (1), and forming a simple 'empty stance' with 60 to 70% of your weight on the rear leg. (A description of the empty stance and knee position is discussed later on page 70.) You are now ready to commence the next backward step (2), or to proceed with a new movement.

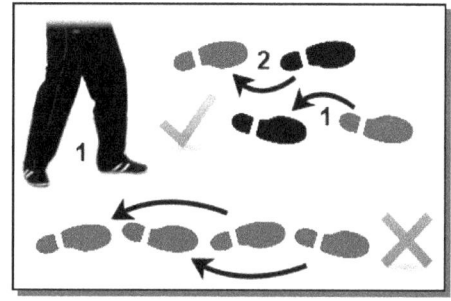

Backward Step (Yang)

Sun Style: In Sun style again the weight is transferred to the static leg and the heel is raised on the stepping leg (unless it is already up from a previous empty stance). Unlike Yang style though the stepping of the moving foot is straight back, as in conventional walking, but the leg should still maintain a small sideways spacing with toes at a slight angle (1). The ball of the foot is placed down first

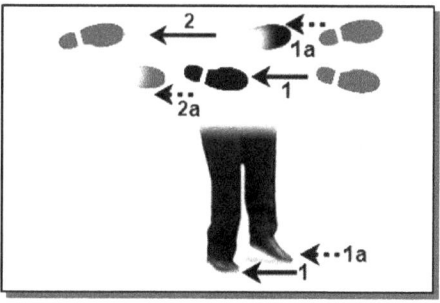

Backward Step (Sun)

Note: Because the Sun Style has a more upright stance, the step distance is shorter than in Yang style.

Once the step distance is set by placing the foot behind, the weight is transferred to the rear leg smoothly via the Dan Tien, rolling the heel down as the foot is placed fully on the floor. The front, now 'empty', leg stays in alignment with the hips, but withdraws (follows through) with a small step (DON'T just lift the heel up) maintaining an upright stance with the ball of the foot (NOT just the toes) braced slightly to the floor (1a) and heel raised slightly. The main centre of gravity is over the rear leg with a small (20-30%) of weight on the ball of the front foot.

You are then ready to carry out a new movement, or continue making further steps back by continuing the forward weight transfer and stepping again (2 & 2a).

All Styles: The back should be kept straight with the pelvis still sitting on the imaginary fence or high stool. The head should be upright and the eyes should remain looking forward and not down at the feet or behind. The knee moves over the toes and never out to the side (as discussed on page 60). Try not to allow the head to bob up and down.

To obtain a bigger backward step whilst maintaining an upright stance, you will soon realise that you will have to sink the supporting rear knee lower to allow the 'free' leg to extend back further - but beginners should stay within their comfort zone and keep their stepping distance to a sensible gap.

Knee Movements

Safe knee movement has been discussed earlier on page 60. Now let's consider the dynamics of how we implement knee movement for Bow and Empty stances in two styles, Yang and Sun.

Forward Bow Stance (Right or Left)

This posture position is an extension to the first rooting movement of the forward step described earlier. It is primarily used in martial practice to deliver a push or punch where the rooted weight is transferred to the forward leg to provide purchase and stability for the action.

Yang Style: In Yang style the front leg is bowed forward with the rear leg braced behind the body, foot angled outwards. Feet must be spaced hip-width apart and NOT positioned directly behind each other. The weight should be distributed approximately 60% to the bowed leg and 40% to the rear leg, and you should feel as if you are sitting on the edge of a fence or high stool.

Sun Style: In Sun style the rear leg still stays spaced hip-width apart, but follows through to maintain a slightly higher stance with the ball of the foot (NOT toes) braced slightly to the floor to the rear and carrying a small (10-20%) of your weight, ensuring that the main centre of gravity is over the forward leg. Again you should feel as if you are sitting on the edge of a fence or high stool.

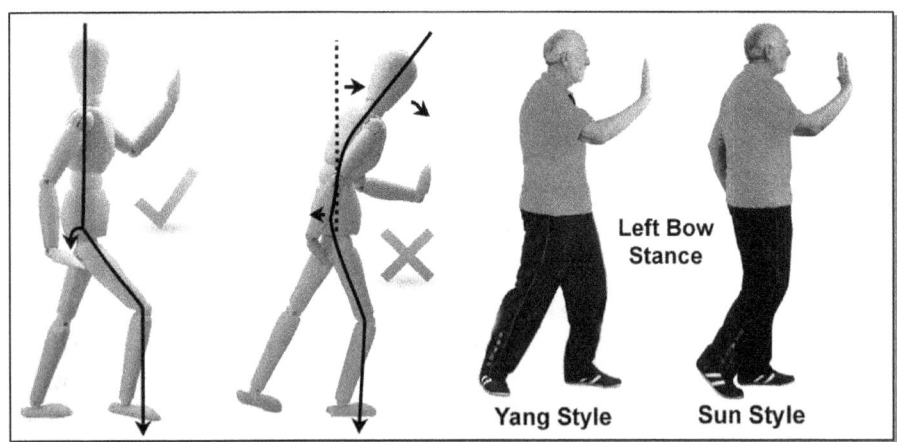

Basic Bow Stance

All Styles: In both cases the back is maintained in a vertical position and the brace point of the movement - the point at which the feet are firmly in position - should be synchronised to occur a fraction before the maximum limit of the hand movement - the contact point of a push or punch - is reached.

Any further forward force from the hand, either pushing or punching would be applied by sinking the pelvis downward towards the ground by bending the knees - and NOT by leaning forward. This will maintain a powerful and stable rooted posture and ensure that you cannot be pushed over backwards or fall forward if an opponent releases any resistance.

Seated: When seated and carrying out this movement, keep the back straight and try to push downwards into the seat of the chair. If you can manage to simulate the bowed leg by applying direct pressure down the one leg that is opposite to the associated hand/arm movement, then do so, but avoid twisting the hip on the other side upwards.

Empty Stance (Right or Left)

This posture position is an extension to the first rooting movement of the backward step described earlier, where weight is transferred to the rear leg by rolling back. It is primarily used in martial practice to provide purchase and stability for blocking or pulling an opponent towards you to destabilise.

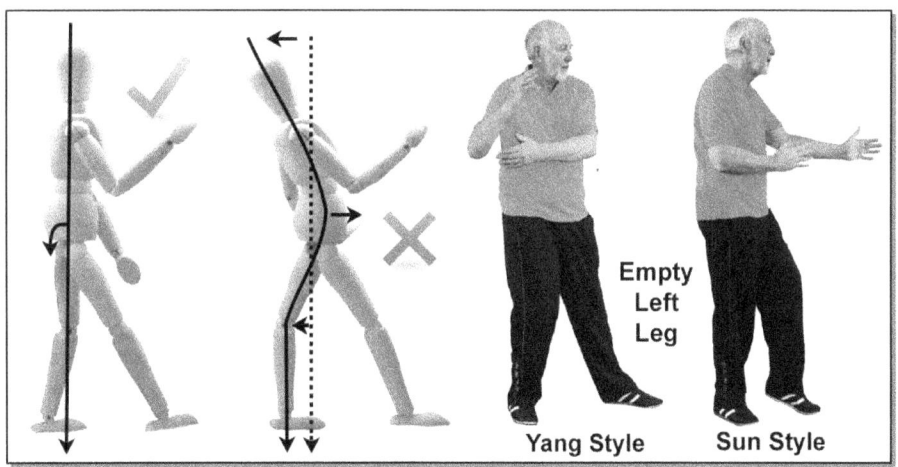

Basic Empty Stance

Yang Style: In Yang style the one leg steps back and the pelvis sinks downwards as if sitting on the edge of a fence or high stool. The legs remain hip-width apart with the front 'empty' leg remaining in a forward position, but straightened by lifting the heel as the weight is transferred to the rear leg by the 'sitting' action of the pelvis. The heel may then be lowered to gain rooted purchase.

Sun Style: In Sun style as in the Yang, the one leg steps back and the pelvis sinks downwards as if sitting on the edge of a fence or high stool. The front 'empty' leg, is then withdrawn to just in front of the body to maintain an upright stance with the heel lifted as the weight is transferred to the rear leg by the 'sitting' action of the pelvis. The front leg still carries a small (10-20%) of weight.

All Styles: In both cases the back is maintained in a vertical position and the end point of the movement - the point at which the feet are firmly in position - should be synchronised to occur a fraction before the maximum travel of the associated hand movement is reached.

Any further pull would be applied by sinking the pelvis downward towards the ground by bending the knees and NOT by leaning backward. This will maintain a powerful and stable rooted posture, ensuring that you will not fall backward if an opponent releases any resistance and moves towards you.

Seated: When seated and carrying out this movement, keep the back straight and try to push downwards into the seat of the chair. If you can manage to simulate the bowed leg by applying direct pressure down the one leg that is opposite to the associated hand/arm movement, then do so, but avoid twisting the hip on the other side upwards.

Simple Turns

The way you turn to left or right will depend upon the T'ai Chi style that you are practising, the overall intent of the movement that you are doing and, most importantly, your mobility. The primary aim must be to turn stably and safely.

Your teacher will demonstrate specific turns and will ensure that you are stable and safe. However, the following notes provide a basic guide to some simple turns to illustrate the principles and for your reference as you practise at home.

Just as there is weight shift and flow in other movements, so too there must be in full stepping turns and also in pivoting turns - turns where no definite step is made. These vary with style, but basically they normally use the heel or toe on an 'empty' or non-weighted leg to initiate a 45 or 90 degree turn. Traditional and martial forms often use direct turns up to 270 degree and spin turns, but these assume agility and correct application in order to avoid injury or strain. Normally for beginners two stage movements with an interim 45 degree turn are taught.

Please note: Elderly beginners or those with balance or joint problems are advised initially to carry out the movements using a conventional step-around movement rather than any heel/toe pivot.

Below are three examples of typical turns that you will meet - a 90 degree stepping turn illustrated as a Yang style movement, a heel and toe turn illustrated in its Sun style variant and a general heel/heel turn.

90 Degree Stepping Turn

The illustration below shows the Yang style version of this turn. *The Sun variant is similar except that there is a follow through 'empty' step with the rear leg.*

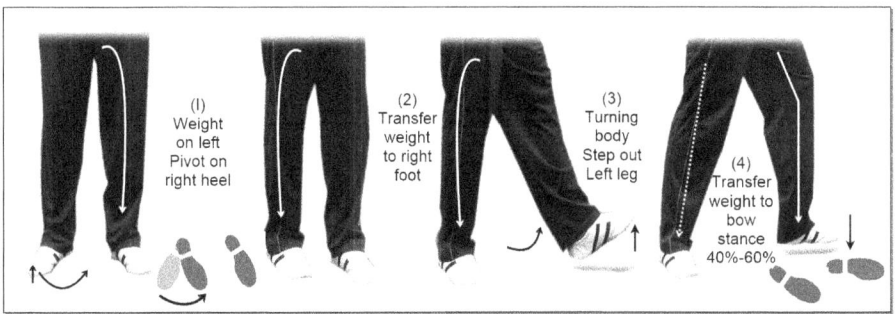

Principle of a 90 degree Stepping Turn to Right (Yang style)

1. From the rooted stance, shift weight to the leg that is on the side of the direction to be turned (i.e turning right shift weight to right leg, turning left shift weight to left leg).

2. Lift the toe on the 'empty' leg and pivot 90 degrees on the heel of that foot to start the turn, softening the knee on the weighted leg. Don't forget correct knee alignment discussed previously on page 74.

3. Transfer the weight back to the other leg.

4. Step the new 'empty leg' in the direction of the turn, placing heel down first.

5. Finally roll weight forward onto that foot to complete a rooted bow stance and the turn. (In Sun style an additional movement is required to 'follow-up' the rear leg to provide the upright stance.)

Heel/Toe Turn

This type of turn (as illustrated) is used quite a lot in Sun style, but is also used with a wider stance in other styles of T'ai Chi.

Assuming that you are turning 90 degrees in a direction towards the existing 'empty' leg

1. Lift the heel on the 'empty' foot. *(In Sun style the heel will already be lifted.)*

78 Simplifying T'ai Chi

2. Pivot on the ball ('*toe*') of the 'empty' foot bringing the heel inwards towards the other weighted heel.

3. Remember to keep the knee aligned over the toe, shift the weight to the 'empty' leg (the one that has just been turned) and lift the toe on the foot which was previously weighted and is now 'empty'.

4. Pivot on the heel of that foot to complete the turn.

5. Shift and even the weight back to form a neutral rooted stance.

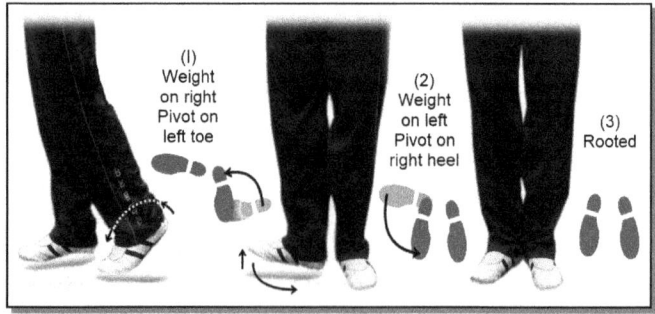

Principles of a Heel/Toe Turn - Right Side to Front (Sun style)

90 Degree (non-stepping) Open Stance Turn to Left

By now you should have started to grasp the idea of using heel and toe pivots applied to an 'empty' leg to complete safe turns. These principles are applied to almost all of the angled turns that you will meet as a beginner. This final example illustrates a non-stepping heel/heel type of turn, and assumes a turn to the left from a wide-legged open stance such as a single whip to punch under elbow in Sun style.

1. With your weight on left leg, lift the toe on the right 'empty' foot and pivot it on the heel in the direction of the turn. Lower the toe.

2. Transfer the weight to sit back on the right leg, and lift the toe on the left foot to pivot the foot on the heel in the direction of the turn.

3. Complete the turn by lowering the left toe and transferring the weight back to

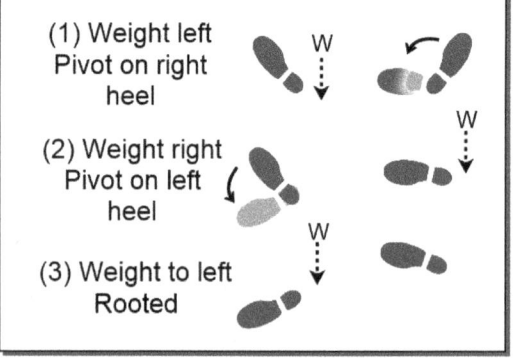

Principles of a Heel/Heel Turn

the forward left leg in readiness for the next (or the remainder of the) form movement.

Spin Turns

Dynamic fast turns which can be up to 360 degrees rotation are encountered in all traditional forms, often to precede a kick. These are definitely NOT for beginners who should NEVER attempt them without initial experienced supervision.

Beginners learning traditional form or those less able should use a slow walk-around, or remain stationary omitting the turn completely.

Kicks

For the beginner kicks are difficult to achieve and perform safely and elegantly. NEVER attempt full kicks until you have been practising T'ai Chi for a while and you have the back-up of a teacher. This is very important if your reason for T'ai Chi is to improve your mobility or other health-related problems.

Even if you are agile, nothing destroys the look of a well performed form more than an inelegant kick with the performer over-balancing or wobbling around. The advice here will ensure that you will look good always remain in control.
The descriptions refer the picture on the next page.

Types of Kick: There are a variety of types/combinations of kicks. Classically kicks can be front or at an angle, high or low, toe or heel, horizontally to the side, leg lifts, spinning or jumping.
Beginners though should initially stick to toe-points or knee lifts.

The Hands: When you are making a kick *(stage 3 in the following descriptions)*, the hands are pushed out to the side, below shoulder height and slightly to the front. This is a key movement for stability especially when learning:

> The hands should coordinate with the kick itself, pushing out with the intent of the kick, not tensing the shoulder up or flapping loosely out like extending wings. Imagine that the hands are pushing equidistantly against the two sides of a door frame. This will vertically align your posture for maximum stability and help you to correctly root downwards on the supporting leg.

Toe (heel) - points: This is the safest way to implement a kick. The procedure for the movement can be broken down into three stages:

> Stage 1: Shift the body weight as described earlier on page 68.
> Stage 2: When you are happy with the weight shift, test your balance by lifting the heel of the 'empty' leg.
> Stage 3: When you are happy with balance - and NOT before - flex the knee and ankle, part the hands and point the toe.

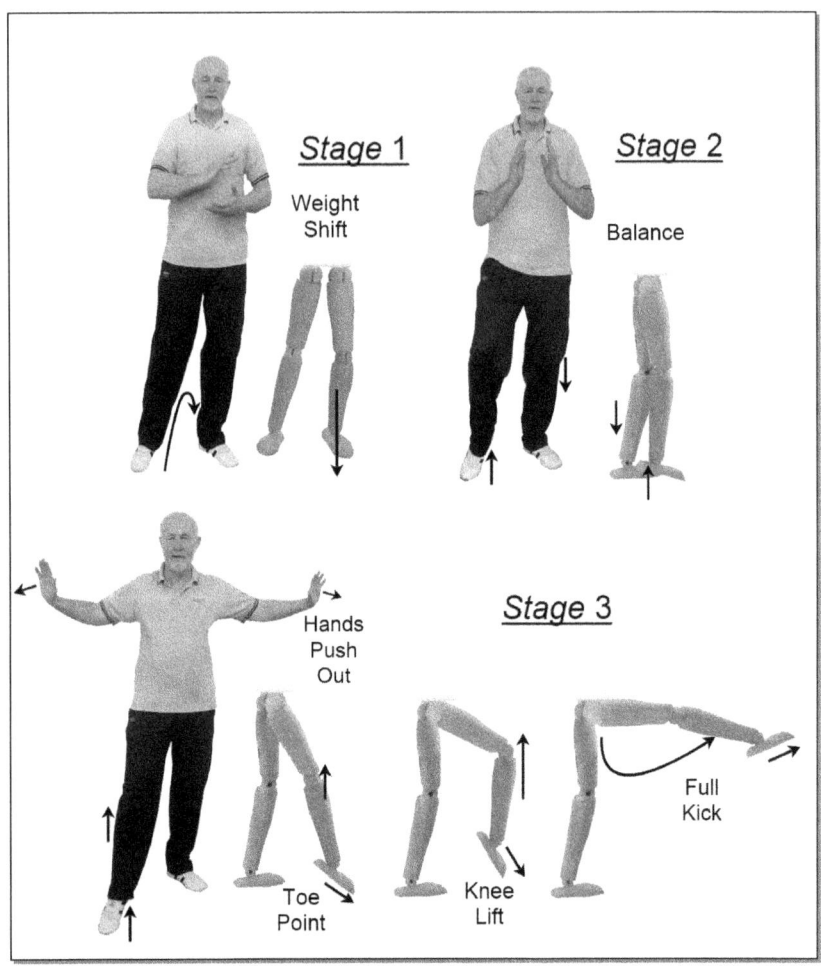

Developing Kicks

Knee Lifts: Once you're happy with balance and toe-points, providing you have good knee movement, you can try knee lifts. The stages for this are:

Stage 1: Shift the body weight as described earlier on page 68.
Stage 2: When you are happy with the weight shift, test your balance by lifting the heel of the 'empty' leg.
Stage 3: When you are happy with balance - and NOT before - part the hands and lift the knee to hold the foot off the floor. Don't try a full kick at this stage.

Full (toe/heel) Kicks: These are best left to learn from your teacher but the principles above still apply. Once you are confident with balance, have mastered the toe-kicks and have good knee movement you're potentially ready for a full kick procedure. This too has three stages:

Stage 1: Shift the body weight as described earlier on page 68.
Stage 2: When you are happy with the weight shift, test your balance by lifting the heel of the 'empty' leg - you can always 'back out' at this stage and convert to a toe point or knee lift.
Stage 3: When you are happy with balance, part the hands and kick.

Kua

Kua is defined as the hip area or more specifically the ball and socket joint of the femur and the pelvis.

It is fundamental to T'ai Chi in that without the Kua the upper and lower body cannot properly work together as the Kua integrates the two and ensures that they work harmoniously together. Other general associations are often made, but in real terms, rotating or sinking the Kua modifies the structure and movement of your body. The better you are at using the Kua, the better your body is coordinated.

OK - so how does that apply to my T'ai Chi? How do I use Kua?

Let's assume that we are standing up and wish to turn our head and shoulders through 45 degrees:

> Assume that we are standing in the classic T'ai Chi starting stance, feet around a foot apart, knees soft and back straight as if sitting on the edge of a fence or high stool.
> We then are asked to turn without moving our feet.
> The normal response for someone with no T'ai Chi background would be to turn the shoulders, leaving the waist and connected legs where they are .... Ouch! ...... yet another potential bad back or slipped disc.
> *There is a set of rules in T'ai Chi known as the Six Harmonies which we'll discuss later on page 89. One of the rules laid down in the three external harmonies relating to the hip and shoulder alignment has been broken.*

Now let's see how it should be achieved. Place your hand with fingers pointing out in front of your navel to act as a pointer to show direction and observe the following:

> Consider the knees as hinges - they can only fold and bend in one direction.
> Consider the Kua as ball joints - they can rotate the femur and hence the leg. With the feet fixed on the floor, bend one knee forward towards (but not over) the toes and see the effect.

As the knee lowers:

> The hip rotates slightly downwards on that side - *Sinking the Kua*.
> The hip on the other side rotates and rises as the weight is released and the leg lengthens slightly - *Opening the Kua*.
> Now observe the pointing fingers.

The body will have rotated through an angle - the wider the initial stance and more the knee bends, the greater will be the turn angle.
Notice too that the shoulders and hip are still in alignment.

This is the meaning of *Sinking* and *Opening* the Kua - rotating the upper body using leg muscles and avoiding a twist of the spine. The term refers to both left or right movement.
Sinking the right Kua and opening the left Kua turns the body to the right.
Returning back to root position closes the Kua.
Sinking the left Kua and opening the right Kua turns the body to the left.

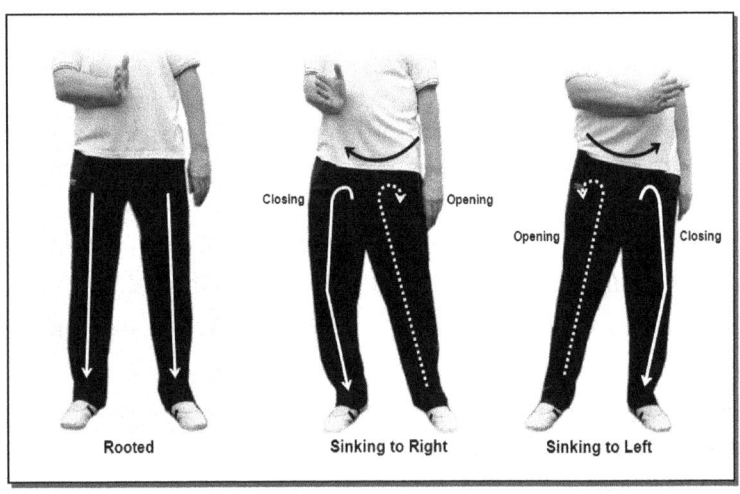

Sinking the Kua

To summarise with a simple analogy, when you are told by your teacher to exercise the Kua, imagine that your head is a mop head supported on a vertical handle or shaft which is your spine. Any rotation of your head or upper body is achieved using the knee, hips and leg muscles, which in practical terms means that the mop head turns and so does the mop handle.
The handle (your spine) doesn't twist!

Another way of thinking about it is to image a log floating in a river. The force of the water moves the log around corners, but the log (your spine) doesn't flex.

The upper body is moved by the rooted force in the legs. The trunk cannot move independently. It can only rotate by adjusting to the action of the legs via the Kua using the knees. When the knee moves, energy is propelled both ways, to the feet through into the ground for stability and to the Kua to turn the trunk and the waist.

Exercising Kua requires that you correctly use the associated body parts - a combination of thigh bones, knees, femurs, hip joint, leg muscles and also your weight and tail bone movement.

Many people confuse *Kua* with *Waist.* The observer sees waist movement but the actual work is done by the knees, leg muscles and hip joint (Kua). The waist itself is considered as part of the upper body or trunk that extends to the shoulders, moving as one like a cylinder, pivoting on the Kua.

Transferring From A Low To A High Stance

This tip is definitely a 'must' for advanced practice, but is included here as it is useful for beginners who often complain that due to weak leg muscles, they have difficulty transferring back up from a low to a higher stance, i.e. transferring from a semi-crouching to a more vertical stance.

The main problem when rising from a rooted 'sunk' position is that with a straight back and forward pelvis, lifting straight up entails direct pressure on the leg muscles as they are lifting the whole upper body weight.

First, recall that we have already said that T'ai Chi has a circular element to its movements. Recall also that when we sank down to a rooted stance the pelvis was rolled forward. It follows therefore that we should again use the pelvis movement to gain assistance for the lift.

When you are standing in the basic *wuji* posture *(on page 65)*, your lower back *(ming men)* should be curved slightly inward to the front and your angled pelvis will be causing your stomach to be curved slightly (only slightly!) out in front. Imagine a ball inside *(Dan Tien)* that is rotating towards your back pushing the stomach outwards.

To rise up we need to reverse this process. Rotate this ball towards the front pulling it backwards to rest on a now horizontal pelvis. This will initiate the lifting movement from the Dan Tien using the stomach muscles, pulling the thighs up and relieving some of the demand on the leg muscles. **Try it!**

Chapter 10
T'ai Chi Harmony

Breathing

Correct breathing is very important for T'ai Chi, but as a beginner you shouldn't concentrate on it so much at the expense of posture and learning a simple form. During your initial learning phase you should just breathe naturally through the nose as you are practising. Master the basic T'ai Chi movement first. It is very noticeable when beginners start to try to incorporate breathing, that they tense up, lose concentration and their movements become jerky. *Your teacher won't want to see you become red or blue in the face either!*

The best way to appreciate and learn breathing technique is to practise simple Qi Gong. You will then soon find that as you do the dynamic T'ai Chi form, you will automatically start to apply Qi Gong breathing techniques to control and pace the movements.

Generally, as all the movements of our T'ai Chi style are based on an in-and-out movement, breathing will become the metronome for your practice. When you are ready to add it to your form, you will gradually learn to take deeper and longer breaths.

The slower the breath count the slower the form. In general as a beginner, breathe in on inward, pulling and settling movements (Yin), gathering Qi. Breathe out on outward, pushing, external movements (Yang) and when expelling Jin energy. Time the movement to your breathing, rather than timing your breathing to your movements.

Ideally to gain maximum health benefit you should develop deep diaphragmatic or lower abdominal breathing (the Taoists call this Yang breathing). Once mastered you will start to experience deeper enhanced feelings of Qi and you will add an internal organ massage factor to the health giving properties of your practice.

Not so important, but good if you can manage it, as you progress, try to adopt a tongue position where the tip is just touching the roof of the mouth. This optimises the airflow passage. Then breathe in naturally through your nose and out through your mouth.

Lower Abdominal Breathing

Ideally one of the first things to try to perfect once you have started to appreciate the initial concepts of T'ai Chi is a breathing skill. You will then start to adopt this when practising, initially with your Qi Gong, and then hopefully with your T'ai Chi form. Experiment and try to learn to breathe deeply into the area below your navel. This is known as Lower Abdominal Breathing or Yang Breathing, and once perfected will maximise the effect of your practice.

We all start our young lives breathing in this way. If you observe sleeping babies and young children you will see that as they breathe 'in' their tummies rise. As we get older most people in the West start to adopt the opposite of this, breathing in a shallow way that only partially utilises lung capacity. This is recognised by the upper chest lifting and expanding on the 'in' breath with the tummy contracting in. On the 'out' breath the reverse happens and the tummy expands and the chest drops. *This type of breathing is said to stimulate the mind - so maybe this is why we automatically adopt it in our formative years.*

'Yang Breathing' is the reverse of this and is characterised by an expansion of the lower abdomen during the 'in' breath. As you inhale, air is pushed downwards sinking the chest expanding the tummy. As you exhale the chest lifts and the tummy contracts inward. Your overall breathing pace is slowed down and deepened as you completely fill your lungs.

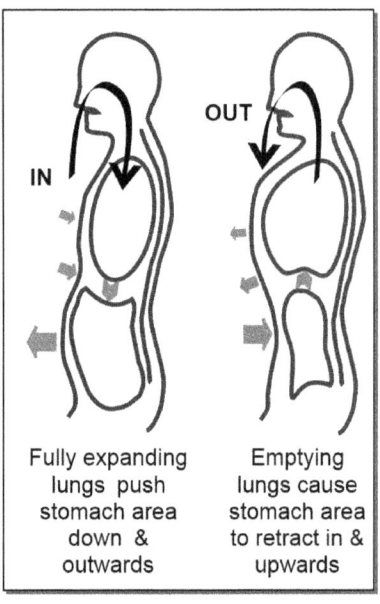

Fully expanding lungs push stomach area down & outwards

Emptying lungs cause stomach area to retract in & upwards

Yang Breathing (Simplified)

This deeper type of breathing not only excites and activates the Qi, but on a physical level it gives you an internal massage by the expansion and contraction of the muscles and the internal organs. It helps to improve blood circulation and liver functions, oxygenates the blood more efficiently, exercises the pelvic floor and spinal 'core' muscles, and generally benefits the body metabolism.

The Philosophy of Deep Breathing

As you breathe deeply you concentrate the mind on the sinking of the breath down to the centre of the body area (the 'Outer Circle') - the body balance point and centre for physical movement located between the hips and navel.

In Chinese philosophy, this is of primary importance, for as well as being the central balance point of the body, it is also the main centre for the storage and circulation of Qi energy. Centralised around 5 cms below and inwards from the navel, this is the Dan Tien, referred to sometimes as the 'Lower Cauldron' or the 'Inner Circle'. It can only be effectively reached and activated by deep breathing.

You can see therefore, that from this perspective, deep controlled breathing is very important for the health of your body, mind and spirit, in both internal and external activities.

Yin & Yang

Whenever you see reference to T'ai Chi you see the Yin & Yang symbol. In so many ways this is considered to be representative of T'ai Chi practice and its philosophy. Here we will consider some of the fundamental, easy to understand concepts of it so that you will start to see how you can use the symbol to improve and relate to your practice.

Let's examine the symbol:

- The black and white circular symbol is divided into two equal tadpole-like components. The black part is referred to as Yin and white part is referred to as Yang.

- Each starts small and increases in size.

- Within the black Yin area there is a white dot. Within the white Yang area there is a black dot.

- Both sides are complementary opposites, yet each contains a small factor of the other (the dot).

- The two parts forming a circle with the serpentine line dividing them create the impression of flowing, circular motion.

- Some of the characteristics attributed to Yin are: female, passive, soft, an energy-charging 'In' breath.

- Some of the characteristics attributed to Yang are: male, active, hard, an energy-expelling 'Out' breath.

So how does Yin & Yang symbolism relate to our basic T'ai Chi practice?

A circular ball with two components

When we start our first T'ai Chi lessons we will most likely be told to consider that the Qi is held in a spherical shape either in the Dan Tien or carried as a ball between the gently curved hands.

Flowing circular movement

All our T'ai Chi movements are flowing and smooth with a circular component. There are no angular movements or extensions in our practice. Hand and arm movement all have a circular component in them and start gently and increase in power.

Balanced opposites

T'ai Chi is full of opposites. Qi is absorbed and expelled by the in and out breath. The body is kept balanced during movement by a rooted or "solid" component and a free moving "empty" component as we move from one leg to another. Each movement has a yin and yang or in and out movement. Force against us is detected and, if it cannot be avoided, is deflected back and returned.

Yin in Yang, Yang in Yin

In T'ai Chi, despite each movement having a dominant yin and yang component, they are never 100%. Each contains an element of the other *(the 'dots')*. Just like the up and down of a car suspension there is a reserve of compression in extension and a reserve of extension in compression. Nothing locks or bottoms out.

Smooth interaction

The serpentine lines of the symbol suggest flowing movement, just like the waves lapping the beach. In T'ai Chi two components are in constant motion, gently pushing and pulling, never stopping, each flowing into the other. Combining the flowing movement with the yin in yang and yang in yin produces gentle unstressed movement of every joint and muscle in the body. *'Silk Reeling' on page 92.*

Powerful action

Once the concepts described above are appreciated, the analogy of controlled force becomes apparent. The waves on the beach can be gentle but also unstoppable, as demonstrated during winter storms, hurricane storms or the ultimate tsunami.

In T'ai Chi we apply the amount of force needed to produce the result required. This is why the softness is felt when practising T'ai Chi as a health exercise, and yet the martial side of T'ai Chi Chuan is often described as being a force where a pound can move a ton, a mouse a mountain.

Six Harmonies

Previously we talked about the Yin and Yang symbol epitomising T'ai Chi movement flow. Another important expression that you will meet is *Six Harmonies*. These summarise the posture and attitude adopted to achieve flowing balanced movement.

The harmonies are split into two groups of three - all six must be in harmony to achieve correct stance and movement.

External harmonies:

- Hips and Shoulders. *San*
- Elbows and Knees. *Wai*
- Hands and Feet. *He*

These three physical attributes provide safe posture and physical strength.

Internal harmonies

- Spirit/Emotion. *Shen, Xin*
- Mind/Intent. *Yi*
- Energy. *Qi*

These three attributes define the mental attitude to produce control and emotional strength - *Li*.

So what do they collectively imply?

Three External Harmonies

The External groups refers to the interaction and unity of movement of the hips and shoulders, elbows and knees, hands and feet. This produces a holistic *(whole-body)* movement where any single part is not effective if the other parts are not moving in harmony. For these parts to move in harmony, they must work as one. In other words if you're making a particular movement, it is only correct if the harmony conditions are met.

For example:

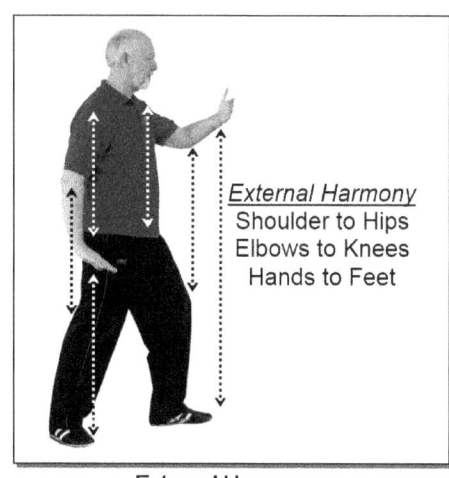

External Harmony
Shoulder to Hips
Elbows to Knees
Hands to Feet

External Harmony

If you're making a turn that involves movement of the hips *(Kua)* the shoulders should remain in alignment (harmonise) with the hips - the trunk appearing as a solid tube, not twisting at the waist or leaning forward. (There's a lot more about Kua on page 81.)

When you make and complete an arm and leg movement, the elbow should be in vertical alignment with the knee. The knee and elbow harmonise.

Similarly your feet harmonise with the hands, both vertically and in direction. i.e. If the hand is moving forward it will be in the direction of the leading foot and be vertically aligned with the toes.

Please note that if you are older or less able, the exact theoretical alignment may not be possible, as age and immobility can restrict movement. The goal however is still there, but always remember the maxim to use only 95% of your available movement.

Remember also though that harmonising is not just about the static position alignment at the end of a movement. There also has to be an overall coordinated harmony and energy flow between the moving limbs. Your feet are invisibly connected through to the hands, your hips through the shoulders, and your knees to the elbows. This means that any particular movement, for example stepping forward into a hand push, uses the foot to push into the ground, spiralling energy up through the knee, hip, via the dan tien to the shoulders, elbow and thence to the hand.

When one part moves - all parts move

For a movement to flow and to be and feel correct, the alignments must be maintained throughout the movement, then you will find that at its completion your elbow will be over the knee, the hand will be over the foot and your shoulders over your hips (not twisted or leaning forward).

This concept will be at the heart of any progressive posture corrections that your teacher will impart to you as you gain more experience.

Three Internal Harmonies

The Internal group, Spirit or Emotion, Mind or Intent and Energy (*Shen, Xin, Yi, Qi*) must also all be harmoniously present and working together. When all three are together Emotional Strength *(Li)* is produced.

This applies to all T'ai Chi whatever the aim - martial or for health.

The spirit *(Shen)* harmonises with the intention *(Yi)*, the intention with healthy energy *(Qi)* and in turn this total combination provides the strength *(Li)*.

In martial terms, if you are attacked and your spirit is weak you will be immediately defeated, or if you are angry your intent will be lost or confused, and you will not be able to use your energy to defend yourself effectively.

For health T'ai Chi, you must want to achieve something *(spirit or motivation)* from your effort *(intent)*. This will then stimulate the power *(energy)* required for healing or improvement *(generated strength)*.

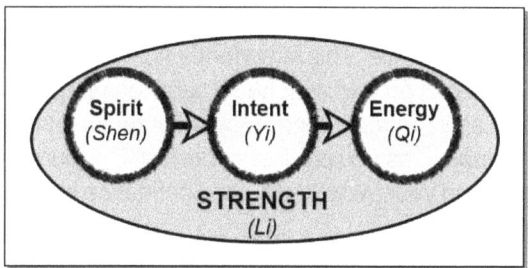

Internal Harmony Provides Inner Strength

In summary, you must have the will to achieve a goal; have the intent to carry it through; so that force required will be generated. Your goal will then be fulfilled. All three internal harmonies are required for effectiveness.

To be effective requires motivation, rational effort, and controlled power

The Six Harmonies Together As One

So how does this apply to T'ai Chi for health exercise?

As we see above, each of the groups, the three internal and three external harmonies, must work together within themselves for effective strength.

The two groups must also work with each other to provide overall strength and effect. The internal requires the external to implement the goal and equally the internal requires the external. This is why those that practise (and teach) T'ai Chi movement aerobically, just copying movement, will never achieve the full benefit - the internal will be incomplete as the intent will be missing, and the external will almost certainly be incomplete because correct alignment will not be there.

The six harmonies are very important from the martial viewpoint, but are equally so when using T'ai Chi in a health regime where the 'self-defence' is against ill-health and 'dis-ease'. You must have a strong spirit to practise properly and overcome and work within your abilities. Your mindset and intention must be clear and focused. Do this and the effect of the healing energy (Qi) will be maximised. Learning to maintain good posture and alignment will improve balance and ensure minimum joint and body stress during movement.

The Six Harmonies will all be working as one

Silk Reeling Harmony

The most obvious characteristic to an observer of those starting to learn T'ai Chi, is the lack of fluidity and smoothness of movement when compared to those who have been practising for a while. This is perfectly normal in beginners, just as it is in any other art. We've probably all watched a baby learning to walk or listened to a child learning to play an instrument, and what about those first driving lessons? Just as in these examples, as you progress your T'ai Chi journey, your posture and movement improves and your awareness and confidence increases.

Throughout this book there have been many references to fluidity and harmony of movement, relating it to flowing water, waves on a beach, animal movement, and to the circular and serpentine movements illustrated by the Yin and Yang symbol described on page 87.

Another term often used to describe the fluid controlled movements of T'ai Chi form is 'Silk Reeling'. This allegorical term relates to the spiralling movements of a silk-worm larva as it forms its cocoon, and the subsequent actions that are required later to unravel it and draw an unbroken thread that can use to create a fabric. Here, the person drawing the thread has to develop a light, smooth unwinding action. There can be no jerking or changing direction - which would break the thread, nor can there be any slackening - which would cause the thread to stick to itself or tangle.

The description of this type of movement is the one that you should endeavour to apply to your T'ai Chi. To do so you must employ all of the 'six harmonies'on page 89. The three external harmonies describe how key parts of the body are related together to provide correct posture and linked together as one unit by the body's connective tissue to provide smooth movement. For example the hand and foot should appear connected and move as if joined together. Similarly, the internal harmonies describe how the non-physical energy control is completed. We can say therefore, that this 'reeling silk' movement is actually just another way of describing focused, six-harmony movement.

The movements of a series of Silk Reeling Qi Gong routines are often taught by teachers to beginners to help develop this smooth, harmonious interaction - *'go with the flow'*, but there is a much deeper aspect to these Qi Gongs that is often never appreciated or developed.

Silk Reeling and Spiralling Energy

Our goal should ultimately be to achieve not only perfect harmony of movement but also to optimise our flow of energy. Not only will we then have controlled physical smoothness, but we will also be able to achieve maximum power transfer.

The maximisation of power transfer by exploiting internal energy movement is an advanced concept, not normally explained to or understood by the novice, but one that it is essential to eventually develop if you are aspiring to understand T'ai Chi practice to a greater depth. Hopefully one day you will decide that the time has come to pursue this deeper understanding more to move a little further on your journey and you will start to investigate the concept of 'Spiralling Energy'. (This spiral rotation is represented in the Yin & Yang symbol by the serpentine separation of the two halves.)

The ability to develop 'Spiralling Energy' is usually taught by exploiting the deeper 'hidden' facets of Silk Reeling Qi Gongs. In this context - *Chan Si Jin(g)* - the Qi Gong exercises are used to promote awareness and control by 'spiralling' the energy through the body to provide power in addition to just a flexible response in your T'ai Chi movements. Such a complex subject really requires a teacher to expand it to suit your progress and is not within the scope of this book for beginners, but the following simplified explanation may seed your curiosity.

Silk Reeling Qi Gong's deeper asset develops the use of power that is created by radiating energy in a spiral in to and out from the Dan Tien for each of your T'ai Chi movements. This focuses every movement and weight shift through the Dan Tien (and physical core muscles) using the body's meridians to transport spiralling Qi energy to the targeted extremity of the body. For each action this triggers a power derived from unified (whole body) muscle, tendon and connective tissue en route. Compare this with simple conventional pushing, pulling and lifting power derived singularly from the active arm or leg components. This unified movement can be observed demonstrated by running or hunting animals.

Traditionally the Silk Reeling Qi Gongs tend to be associated with the teaching and application of Chen style T'ai Chi. However on analysis, they are just as applicable to all styles of T'ai Chi (and many other martial arts), as all employ these techniques to be effective. When used in this role, the Qi Gongs are supplemented by practising 'Push(ing) or Sticky Hands' with a partner (mentioned on page 50) in order to learn to develop the control of the effect and power of the spiralling energy.

We have already discussed how to achieve basic posture and movement in Chapter 9 where great emphasis was made about weight shift and direction of force (power). All the diagrams used have lines showing the direction and controlled transfer of weight and force. Note that all the lines appear to start or pass through the Dan Tien. Unlike these simplified diagrams though, the more advanced students of T'ai Chi will be taught that the energy does not travel straight from the Dan Tien but circles into it and out from it to the point of application in a rotating spiral along the meridians. Focusing the mind on this spiral will maximise energy flow and power transfer. Each of the in and out spiral movement is coordinated with breathing.

Can a Beginner Develop Spiralling Energy?

As I've already said, Spiralling Energy is an advanced concept and there can be no substitute for a teacher, but if you are familiar and happy with the feeling of Qi and energy movement there are ways that you can to start to initially investigate it. However, whatever you do don't let it hold you back or dominate your practice, you may not yet really have reached the right point in your journey.

- **In your Qi Gongs**. For example the Five Element Qi Gong described later in this book on page 112, you can attempt to spiral the energy into and out of the Dan Tien with each movement and see if you feel any difference.

- **In your T'ai Chi form** there are many example where, if you are ready to, you can initially investigate by carefully attempting to introduce Spiralling Energy into a movement:

In a basic hand movement (punch, block, push, etc.) allow the Dan Tien to gain (reel) energy from the initially rooted foot (or feet), amplify it, and then simultaneously spiral it out radially both to the stepping foot to create a new downward root, and to the point of the application of power - the hand.

Similarly in a kick allow the Dan Tien to reel energy from the foot that is about to kick, amplify it, and then simultaneously spiral it out radially both down to the other foot to create a solid root to the ground, and to the point of the application of power - the kicking foot.

The Harmony of Five Elements

During your T'ai Chi journey you are bound to come across references to the five symbolic elements - Earth, Metal, Water, Wood and Fire.

The ancient Chinese explained the mysteries of the universe and life in general by reference to Yin and Yang and the condensing of key points into five categories, *Five Elements*, and as such these appear in martial arts such as T'ai Chi and also in Qi Gong, Chinese medicine, philosophy, literature and many less obvious disciplines.

You will find an example of this in the names used in the Qi Gong that I have included in this book on page 111.

However, because of the complex and hypothetical relationships that have evolved over the centuries, I always tell beginners not to worry too much about trying to comprehend the philosophical logic of these allegorical terms. I debated the need to even mention them at all in this book but, because you will undoubtedly meet references to them, I proffer the simplified explanation that I usually give when asked, and include the 'standard' universal diagrams.

Chapter 10 T'ai Chi Harmony 95

If you want more explanation and deeper analysis, there are many texts around that attempt to explain them from different perspectives.

I think of the 'five elements' as five boxes which could equally be labelled *A, B, C, D, E*. The contents of these boxes contain five key terms that are applicable to the subject to which the principles are being applied and not just earth, metal, water, wood and fire, e.g. they could be colour, times of day, body organs, seasons (the Chinese add late summer), stepping directions (earth is centred - no step), moods, - the list is endless.

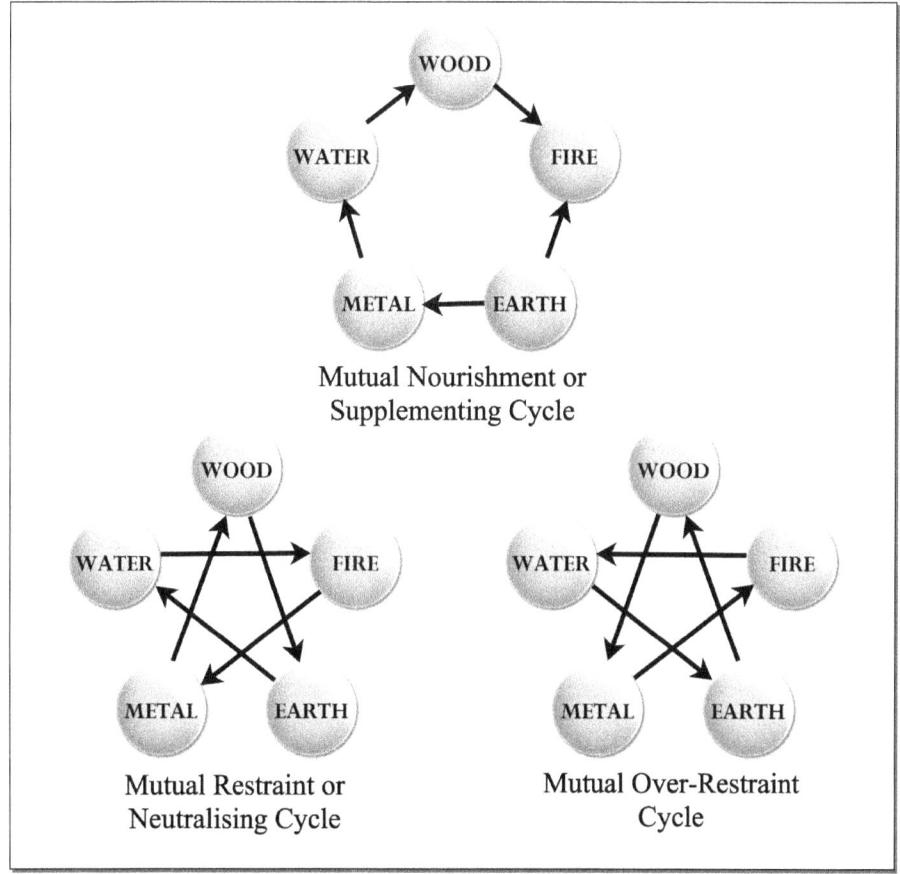

The Key Five Element Cycles

The relationships between the boxes (and thence their content terms) work in several ways. The diagrams shown here use the basic terms of earth, metal, water, wood and fire, but these can be replaced with other terms depending upon the discipline being applied. However, whatever terms referred to, the relationship between the boxes remains true.

Mutual Nourishment or Supplementing relationship *Mother/Son cycle*
Here the connecting term promotes the next until the cycle is completed.

e.g. Water nourishes Wood (a tree) which then grows; Wood in turn feeds a Fire; a Fire creates ashes that add to the Earth; Earth provides the ore to produce Metal; Metal melts and generates fluidity (like water) or is impervious and holds water (a metal vessel).

Mutual Restraint or Neutralising relationship *Win/Lose cycle*
Here the cycle is such that each term checks or restrains the next.
e.g. Water dampens or extinguishes Fire; Fire melts Metal; Metal (axe, knives) cut Wood; Wood (tree roots or wooden tools) displaces or digs up Earth; Earth absorbs or restrains Water.

Mutual Over-Restraint relationship *Encroachment cycle*
If the receiving element is too powerful, or the delivering element too weak, then a temporary reverse-process occurs.
e.g. if a Fire is too fierce or there is not enough Water, the Fire will grow and the Water will evaporate; if Water (a river) flow is too strong it destroys Earth (the river banks); if Earth is too hard or rocky it will damage Wood tools or restrict tree growth; if Wood is too hard it blunts Metal tool blades; if Metal surrounds a Fire it will contain and limit it.

Things can get more complicated with other cycles being defined, especially when applied to traditional Chinese medicine where the elements are defined as Earth - stomach/spleen; Metal - lung/large intestine; Water - kidney/bladder; Wood - liver/gall bladder; Fire - heart/small intestine.

The Message Five Elements Gives to Beginners

For me the most important key message offered by the Five Elements to beginners (and not just when referred to form practice) is:

- That every aspect of T'ai Chi (and everything that you do at other times) should have a natural and positive effect on another.

- That missing out a stage of a movement (and taking short cuts in life) will have a negative effect on the next stage of development of the movement.

- That each movement (and every aspect of your life) should be balanced and controlled. Excessive movement or effort will negate the next movement by causing an instability.

Five Steps & Eight Energies (13 Postures)

Traditional teaching refers to 'Thirteen Postures' which cover the basic movement aspects of classical T'ai Chi. These are comprised of 5 'Steps' which relate to the directions of movement when performing a form, and 8 'Energies' or 'Gates' which relate to the power *(Jin energy)* movements of the form.

Remember that this book has been written to simplify T'ai Chi for beginners and not to teach T'ai Chi in depth, nor is it to investigate the martial application of the movements, and so, apart from 'spiral energy', no real mention has been made of the external energy *(Jin)* that the movements of the form can develop.

It is inevitable that as your practice evolves it will become rather obvious that the movements of the form have direction and complete pushes, punches, throws, etc. To clarify awareness of this and to show you how your movements relate to different categories of movement and force, I'm including a list of these 'Five Steps' and 'Eight Energies' as a reference that you can use if you want to start to study depth of T'ai Chi.

As most of you reading this book will be embarking on using T'ai Chi in its health concept, please do not consider that the following descriptions is in anyway an attempt to introduce martial force to your practice. However, an appreciation of the generic reason for a movement will definitely help to improve your posture control and stance.

Five Steps

When performing your T'ai Chi form you will be moving in four primary directions from a central point. Although these are often just categorised simply as north, south, east and west, the Chinese refer to them as follows, and also relate them to the five elements that form the heart of Chinese philosophy and Qi Gong *(described on page 94)* .

- **Stepping Forward** - *Jin Bu* - Metal.
- **Stepping Backward** - *Tui Bu* - Water.
- **Stepping and Looking Left** - *Zuo Go* - Wood.
- **Stepping and Looking Right** - *You Pan* - Fire.
- **Centred and Static** - *Zhong Ding* - Earth.

Eight Energies

As you progress to a deeper advanced understanding of T'ai Chi, even though you do not intend to pursue the martial perspective, a comprehensive study with an experienced teacher into the meaningful depth of the eight concepts of applying forceful energy will greatly enhance your understanding and outlook of the philosophy and wisdom of T'ai Chi.

At a simplified level for this book, there are eight basic ways that a completed T'ai Chi movement can be used to apply force, referred to by the Chinese as *Eight Energies, Techniques or Gates*, (normally symbolised by the eight trigrams of the classical work *I Ching*). These movements are listed below and in order to illustrate their typical application I've included a few examples taken from Yang style form, but all styles have similar characteristic actions.

- **Lifting** - *Peng* - These movements expand outward to destabilise an opponent and are sometime referred to as 'ward off'.
e.g. Ward Off movement of Yang style 'Stroking Birds Tail'.

- **Diverting** - *Lu* - These movements are of a contracting nature that draw in or redirect an opponent to the side and may be referred to as 'stroking' or 'roll back'.
e.g. Roll-back movement of Yang style 'Stroking Birds Tail', and 'Cloud Hands'.

- **Pressing** - *Ji* - These movements apply force parallel to the floor and horizontally press directly into an opponent to gain some space and turn a situation around to your advantage.
e.g. Lifting (pressing) movement of Yang style 'Stroking Birds Tail'.

- **Pushing** - *An* - These movements apply a more powerful force than the previous press, exerting a strong push to de-stabilise an opponent and move him out of your space.
e.g. Pushing movement of Yang style 'Stroking Birds Tail' and 'Fair Lady Works Shuttles'.

- **Pulling Down** - *Cai* - These movements grab and pull an opponent down towards the ground.
e.g. Yang style 'Needle at the Bottom of the Sea'.

- **Splitting** - *Lie* - These movements are a based on a horizontal rotation movement and used to 'throw' your opponent away from you to the side, often using the leg to as a pivot or trip.
e.g. Yang style 'Parting the Horses Mane', 'Diagonally Flying' and 'the Big Bird Spreads Its Wings'.

- **Elbowing** - *Zhou* - These movements apply a direct strike powered from the elbow. Primarily used in situations where your opponent is attempting to close you in, restricting your manoeuvrability.
e.g. Yang style 'Fan Back', 'Diagonal Flying' and 'Single Whip'.

- **Butting** - *Kao* - These movements are intended for the tightest of spaces and are an extension to the previous Elbow strike. They normally apply to a shoulder strike but can also mean a strike with one or more parts of the body such as chest, back or hips.
e.g. Yang style 'Diagonal Flying'.

Chapter 11
Maxims For Enjoyable Safe Practice

General Movement Maxims

Always remember to follow the basic movement and posture guidance for standing, stepping, sinking the Kua, etc., together with the maxim of the Six Harmonies. This will help to ensure that your practice will be always safe and enjoyable.

When you are moving from one stance position to another, try to maintain an even, level height and avoid bobbing up and down, and don't lean when moving backward or forward.

Above all maintain good posture and be aware of it. Don't rush any movement. Perfect your movement, harmonising with your posture, stance and breathing. Feel the essence that this combination contains.

As you learn your T'ai Chi you will discover that there are many other factors relating to movement. Here are some of them.

Focused and Calm – Empty Mind

When you perform T'ai Chi you should be focused and calm. Many beginners think that this means just forgetting about work or the kids and dreaming about a forthcoming holiday. No it doesn't. T'ai Chi is a disciplined art and requires concentration.

When you start a session the first thing you must do is to empty your mind to rid yourself of the distractions of daily problems. Then, using the deep breathing of Qi Gong, start to focus on each breath, loosening your joints and becoming aware of the build up of Qi. It is this focus that creates a link between your mind and the internal organs as your breathing oxygenates free-flowing blood and the diaphragm movement massages the other internal organs.

Concentrate on your body and the form - not the problems of the world!

Relaxed and Soft

When we perform T'ai Chi the body should be relaxed and soft throughout each movement. This doesn't mean that the body should be sloppy and collapsed. On the contrary the body is kept supple by the flexible open joints and the strength firmly rooted through the legs.

As you move remember the Six Harmonies described on page 89. Focus on the joints that are being used and create intention into each action. This initiates the softness of the movement and links your mind's intention to body movement.

Remember the elastic band analogy.

Concentration

Apart from having to think to remember the movement we are doing...and the next...and the next, we have said that as we move we need to focus on the joints and limbs that are being used and create intention *(yi)* for each action. To achieve this your mind must be alert, active and focused. You have to concentrate as you move.

This is why we say that T'ai Chi is a complete mind and body exercise.

Slowness

All T'ai Chi movements when practised for health benefits should be done slowly to avoid stress or shock damage and to improve coordination. As you learn and practise more your movement will slow and you will start to coordinate your breathing with each Yin and Yang movement.

You will soon develop better muscle control and be able to pay greater attention to each position. Your calmness and patience will improve and you will start to feel the real inner calmness of T'ai Chi. In turn this will encourage you to strive further towards progressive improvement in movement and posture.

An added advantage of slow movement when you are learning is that your teacher can assess slow movement better to see if you are having difficulty, and then make suggestions to adjust or compromise movements that you cannot achieve.

Some advanced T'ai Chi practice does require speed. Even if this is your goal, don't rush. Perfect the movement and harmonise it with your posture, stance and breathing. Feel the essence that it contains. Only then will you have the control to work at any speed you wish.

Slowness develops improvement.

Spontaneity and Natural Movement

The original T'ai Chi movements are reputedly built around observation of animal movements.

Watch how a cat moves – its gentle balanced walk, its slow deliberate but loose movement as it hunts. Watch other animals and see how they control their bodies holistically – no part of the body moves in isolation.

Watch the average westernised human with their jerky stressful movements, clumping down their feet and wearing out hips and knees as they dash from one place to another, damaging their backs as they suddenly twist to pick up an object.

Watch someone who practises T'ai Chi. Observe their 'natural' posture and movement, head held upright, back straight, arms loosely held at the sides. How smooth their movement looks with their joints moving loosely together without tightness.

Develop the control, softness and sure-footedness of a hunting animal.

Coordination

When we perform our T'ai Chi we do it in a holistic way, coordinating upper and lower body movement. I always say that the mind leads the legs and feet; as they move they lead the hands and arms, stimulating a query to the mind 'what is next?'

This combination of uninterrupted body synchronisation will allow smooth, not jerky, movement, and maximise stability, balance and strength.

Let the body move as one like flowing water.

Rooted and Sunk

Once you understand the concept in T'ai Chi of balance and of relaxation, you can think more about the concept of rooting and sinking. In simple terms this refers to the dropping of your centre of gravity by releasing the tension in the back of the knees, straightening the spine by moving the hips slightly forward, and then lowering the Qi energy to the lower abdomen (Dan Tien). This lowering of the centre of gravity improves balance and relaxes the body and all of its joints.

Once sunk the body will gain its strength and stability as with a tree, where the root and trunk are analogous to the feet and legs. The upper half of the body will be flexible and yielding, yet strong, as are the branches of a tree.

All movement will also pivot around this centre of gravity – the Dan Tien – maintaining a stable response with the left arm balancing the right leg and vice versa, the front balancing the back, etc.

Like a tree - a solid trunk, rooted deep, with strong moving branches.

Balance

The basic concepts of T'ai Chi, symbolised by the symbol of Yin and Yang, is one of balanced movement and harmony and actioned by the rooted stance.

As a teacher it is so rewarding when, after only a few weeks we start to see the changes in someone's balance and posture. It is even more rewarding when they recognise it too and tell you of the improvements themselves. This is why T'ai Chi is so useful to help those with debilitating illness such as arthritis, osteoporosis, MS, diabetes, etc. all of which affect balance.

To generalise a little deeper, consider leg movement. The foot that does not carry the body weight is considered Yin, while Yang refers to the foot that does carry the body weight. When it is time to move and you want to move the left foot, you shift your body weight onto the right foot, releasing the left foot and leg for free movement (and vice-versa). This softness of the moving limb minimises the possibility of damage by stress or jarring.

Hand movements will harmonise with foot movement, the hip joints with shoulder joints, and the elbow with the knee joints. Inner energy balance occurs with the harmonising of the mind (thought) and breathing as you execute the movements.

Balance the physical and mental, the whole body with the mind.

Empty and full

You are considered empty and full when you are simultaneously Yin and Yang. Classically you are only said to really start to understand T'ai Chi when you fully appreciate Yin and Yang.

Summarising this simply for the beginner, the concept embraces all the factors that contribute to life, cocooning them into opposite yet attached objects, ideas or forces; one cannot exist without the other.

The two are always in a struggle to overcome each other and harmony is reached when the two components are balanced. Thus with a constant gentle change of position, Yang becoming Yin and Yin becoming Yang.

As you learn, the philosophy of T'ai Chi will start to affect your whole life...

- Your form movements will be balanced, soft and hard; your breathing, both in and out, will be equal.

And then you will maybe notice that...

- Your views will mellow and be moderate and balanced.
- Your diet will moderate and be sufficient without starvation or excess.
- You will start to give time equally to yourself and to others.

The list is endless - your life will be Empty and Full - balanced!

Summary of Best Practice

- *Slowly slowly*

Try to execute all movements as slowly as possible.
Concentrate on each move to get it as precise as possible. Do NOT rush through. Try and visualise the resulting moves and the joints which are involved in producing them.

- *Enjoy your T'ai Chi*

Don't get so serious that you start to worry about the movements when you are practising on your own - the sessions with your group or teacher will provide the necessary correction.
I tell all my students that when on their own they should concentrate on the movements that they are familiar with - it doesn't matter about the order - concentrate on flow and balance.
Just as T'ai Chi form is performed slowly, the learning of the art also proceeds slowly.
It takes time and practice to combine posture, sequence and strength.

- *Visualise Yin & Yang*

All movements should flow smoothly from one to another with gentle rotation and without noticeable pause.

- *Remember the Rooted Tree concept*

Ensure that your upper body is relaxed and loose at all times. Don't forget though that the strength of T'ai Chi is based upon the legs and these, especially the thighs, will undoubtedly ache until strength is built up.

- *Remain aware of posture*

Remember to keep an awareness of your posture and weight transfer at all times.
Keep head up, eyes focused on your out-stretched hand, chin tucked in comfortably.
Ensure chest is relaxed, abdomen pulled in, coccyx pulled in and upward.
Avoid bobbing up and down when moving from one position to another. Try to maintain an even, level height.
Don't twist the waist - sink the Kua.

- *Don't hurt yourself*

To avoid potentially serious damage to the knee joint, never transfer weight onto a leg that does not have the foot, knee and hip in alignment, and never angle a knee joint so far forward that it is in front of the toes.
Ensure that your foot is pointing in the direction that you are facing or going to face BEFORE you transfer the weight.
Never drop the foot down, place it carefully and deliberately.

- **Remain loose - Let Qi flow**

When you extend the arm or punch ensure that there is no tension or lockout.

Keep fingers loose when the hand is open to maximise Qi. *Feel the tingling in your fingers*.

When making punches keep the fist loose, thumb outside, and make any wrist twist at the start of the punch movement not the end.

- **Be aware of your breath**

Always try to breathe in naturally through your nose and out through your mouth. Don't worry too much about the controlled breathing until you are more experienced.

Practise and improve your breathing technique by doing some Qi Gong.

- **If you have a simple illness**

It is best not to practise T'ai Chi when you are suffering an acute illness like influenza or an upset stomach. It is much better to wait until you are recovered.

- **Distraction**

Empty the mind of problems and try not to be distracted when practising. Oh and of course don't forget to turn off your mobile phone!

and above all ...... HAVE FUN!

CHAPTER 12
INTRODUCTORY PRACTICE

Just To Get You Started

I wrote this book to show the beginner how to enjoy safe T'ai Chi, not teach specific T'ai Chi form. The only way to learn form correctly is with a teacher.

However, hopefully, this book will have helped to clarify some points, even more so if you are using other options such as some of the excellent videos and books available, and where you have no teacher to ask.

This section is included first to illustrate how to warm up, and then to provide a simple Qi Gong and examples of some typical Sun and Yang form movements to enable a beginner to start to develop an awareness of Qi, basic posture, balance and movement.

The routines provided are NOT intended to teach you T'ai Chi form or specific style, but to help you to practise a few basic movements when your teacher is not around and enable you to appreciate the things that you've been shown.

A Quick Reminder

When practising at home it's always good to keep checking that you are working safely, so here again is a brief summary of key movement and posture points to remind you before you start.

- Are you sure that you are well enough, relaxed, warmed up and ready for your practice?

- Good posture: knees soft, pelvis tilted slightly forward, coccyx pulled forward and down, chest and shoulders relaxed, chin tucked in, eyes focused on the outstretched hand.

- Relaxed forearms and elbows, 'birds egg' under the armpits, hands and fingers loose and open. Any clenched fists with the thumb outside.

- Movements: slow and continuous, the whole body relaxed and flowing. Synchronise the head, arms, hands, torso, legs, and feet.

- As you move ensure weight shift is balanced and even, maintaining constant head height.

108 *Simplifying T'ai Chi*

- Forward knee movements: always towards, but not beyond your toe and never sideways.
- Work within your abilities - don't overdo things.

Carry on you're doing fine........

A Reminder of Your General Posture

Warming Up

As with any exercise program, before you start your T'ai Chi you should always prepare yourself with a 'warming up' routine.

All teachers will have there own sequences that they prefer to use and I am no exception. Some, particularly those teaching traditional T'ai Chi to fit and active participants, will choose quite vigorous movement, while others who are teaching elderly or disabled, may choose a few very gentle Qi Gong type movements. It is not my intention here to provide you with a set of dogmatic movements, rather to offer a little guidance.

The basic sequence that we follow in all our sessions can be broken down into the following categories but I leave the actual movements to your teacher.

1. **Relax and calm the mind. Forget about the stresses of the day.**

    An ideal way to do this is to walk around slowly and loosely with gentle steps for a minute or so. As you walk roll the head a little, waggle the shoulders and clench/unclench your fists. Breathe deeply, clear your mind and let your body unwind.

2. **Open the joints.**

    Stand (or sit) with your feet slightly apart with no tension in the knees and progressively open your major joints, mentally 'exploding' them to push the joint apart and loosen it. This can take less than a minute or you can slow down the progression to take 5 minutes ... 10 minutes ... whatever.

    Start with the neck, then shoulders and progress down each arm into the fingers. Move down the length of the spine. You should by now start to feel 'inflated' and calm - maybe your fingers are tingling as well. Now progress down the leg joints to the toes. At this point you may feel as if you are standing on rubber - in contact with the ground yet curiously slightly above it.

3. **Progressively move and extend the body, head and limbs.**

    Now that the body has been loosened internally by the previous steps, it is time to extend the movement range. As I said above the movements used are many and varied, but basically in my sessions we start to gently move head and neck and work down the body to the legs with progressive extension over 3 to 5 repetitions of each movement. *We prefer to do these as a Qi Gong, coordinating our breathing with the movements.*

    Typically the sequence should include:

    An initial 'whole body' stretch.
    Head movement up and down then side to side.
    Shoulder rotation.

Arm circular lifts above head.
Arm, shoulder, wrist extension to side and up/down.
Hip (Kua) movement.
Knee movement.
Leg extension.
Knee lifting, ankle, and toe flexing - such as toe points or gentle kicks.
A final 'whole body' stretch and loosening up.

You should now be ready to start and enjoy your T'ai Chi.

Cooling Down

I hate this term when its used in a T'ai Chi context - we're already calm!

Generally with all exercise, a little stretching is recognised as providing better retention of the flexibility derived from any practice. With T'ai Chi, certainly when practised for health, another factor may be added in. After the calming nature of the session, when you have finished you will need to return to the real world.

This doesn't mean that you tense back up and adopt any tight state of mind that you had before you started. On the contrary you should now feel more stable and in control of what life is generally putting your way. Unfortunately one of the side effects, especially for beginners, is that a general sense of calmness and euphoria may be created which for some can be akin to a mild sedative. This is not an ideal state to be in to drive home!

To retain the gained flexibility and to safely continue with the day's activity or drive home it is advisable to carry out a few simple 're-awakening' movements at the end of a session.

>Typically these would consist of a few minutes carrying out several repeats of each of the following:
>
>*Lift each knee in turn to a comfortable height and gently tap the lifted thigh with the side of a clenched fist.*
>
>*Breathing in, clench your hands and contract all your muscles. (Lift onto your toes as well if you can). Relax as you exhale (and lowering heels back to floor).*
>
>*Inhale, lifting the arms slowly upward and outwards to above your head in a curve. Exhale as the arms pull down the centre of the body.*

A Simple Introductory Qi Gong

Start to perfect your breathing technique using this simple Qi Gong which can be done seated or standing. This is a very basic breathing exercise, but you will benefit from doing it daily several times. You should also get into the habit of using this to provide a boost whenever you feel tired and run down

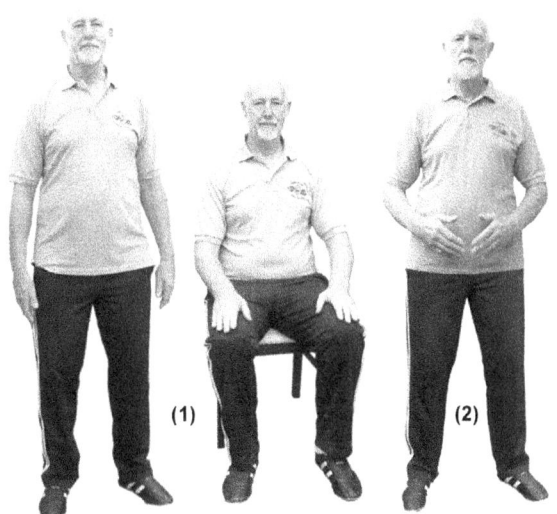

1. Standing: place the feet slightly apart and ensure that your knees are 'soft' not locked in tension. Allow your arms to fall loosely by your side.

Seated: make sure that you have a firm, comfortable chair, ideally without arms, and with a height that allows your feet to be flat on the floor with your upper leg horizontal, knees apart not locked in tension. Place your hands flat on your upper legs. Keep your body fairly upright but without stiffness.

2. Allow your shoulders to drop as low as they will go. Notice that your chest will depress slightly, but don't worry about it, it is quite natural.

3. Free your body and mind from outside influences and internal tensions and place your hands flat on your abdomen.

4. Begin by taking a deep inward breath through the nose, but instead of letting the air fill your lungs and chest, allow your breath to sink so that your abdomen swells outward.

5. Exhale through the nose, allowing your abdomen to draw back inwards, expelling the stale air through your nostrils. Initially assist this by pressing your hands against the abdomen.

6. Repeat at least six times per session.

A Simple Static Qi Gong '5 Element'

This simple Qi Gong, known to us as a 'Five Element Qi Gong' is used at the beginning of all my sessions after the warm up to cultivate an internal focus. It is a very intense internal Qi Gong, ideal to both alleviate stress and to move and feel Qi, and can be carried out seated or standing (or even lying down). Practising is not confined to a T'ai Chi session and so it can easily be used on its own at any time you feel the need:

Stressed at work - do it at your desk.
Can't sleep - do it laying in bed.
Kids playing up - turn your back.
Gridlocked in the car or just waiting - get out if you can, if not, do it as you sit.

Each movement is accompanied by deep breathing (ideally through the nose with the tongue on the roof of the palette) utilising the full range of your diaphragm to breathe - each 'in' and 'out' breathe moving the lower abdomen. ('Yang Breathing' - *In* expands the stomach - *Out* contracts the stomach.)

Static Qi Gong '5-Element' Carried Out Standing or Seated

Five Element Qi Gong Movement Sequence

This is used to provide mental relaxation and general well-being. Carry out a posture with 3 or 5 repeats before moving on to the next in order to experience and control Qi. Although shown standing, it can also be practised sitting or lying down.

Commencing

If standing, adopt the basic standing T'ai Chi posture:

1. Feet apart about shoulder width head up – as if pulled up by an invisible string; chin slightly pulled in; fingers gently curved and slightly apart; tail-bone dropped down; knees as soft if possible (slightly forward, no tension).

2. Breath deeply, cleanse the mind, but think and focus on the movements being done.

3. Ideally use a slow breath count - 'In': *1, 2, 3, 4* - 'Out': *1, 2, 3, 4*

First Posture (Earth)

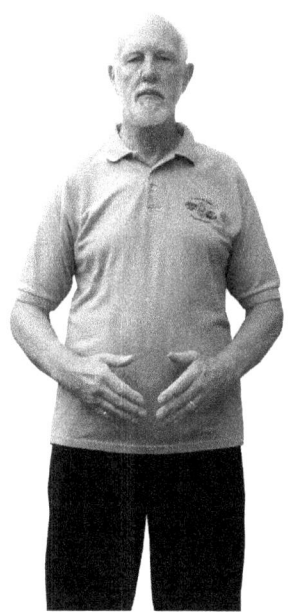

1. Place hands palms over and facing the Dan Tien.
2. Focus on sinking Qi to the Dan Tien.
3. Hold position, breathing slowly and deeply.
4. Each complete breath counts as one exercise.

Second Posture (Metal)

Here feel the focus on the expansion and contraction of the hands as if pulling and compressing a metal spring.

1. Lift the hand into a 'praying' position wrists at mid-chest height. Do not touch the hands together.

2. As you breathe in, slowly expand hands, pulling against an imaginary spring (Qi energy).

3. As you breathe out, slowly compress the hands, pushing against an imaginary spring.

4. Each complete breath counts as one exercise.

Try not to move the hands beyond shoulder width on the expansion or touch them together on the compression. This movement is the one that usually first introduces beginners to Qi as their hands start to feel warm and fingers tingle.

Third Posture (Water)

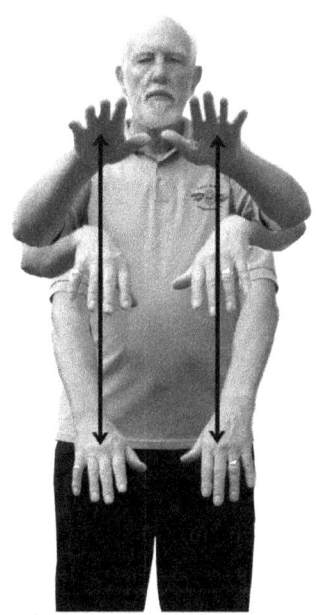

Imagine there is a helium filled balloon (or a water fountain) under your hands.

1. Turn the hands palm downwards and lower them so that the wrists are just below the Dan Tien.

2. As you breathe in, slowly lift hands palms down until at or just below shoulder height. Lead with the wrists so that fingers droop. Simultaneously straighten knees a little if you can (but don't lock them).

The balloon (or water fountain) lifts the hands.

3. As you breathe out, slowly bring hands back down whilst simultaneously bending knees back to the original soft position. Again lead with the wrists so that now the fingers will point at an upward angle. (For a more intense Qi Gong if possible bend the knees to go a little lower but don't push the knees out beyond the toe line.)

Feel the resistance of the balloon (or water fountain) when pushing down.

4. Each complete breath counts as one exercise.

This movement will introduce beginners to Qi sensitivity and control, balancing lightness of yin movement (upward) with the effortless force of yang movement (downward).

Fourth Posture (Wood)

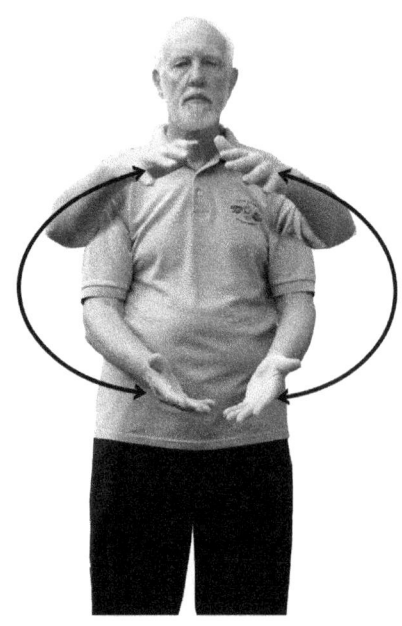

During this posture concentrate on growing the Qi.

1. Turn the palms upward, finger tips around Dan Tien height.

2. As you breathe in, lift arms in an outward curving circular motion describing a circle as if rolling around a large sphere and finishing with the fingers and wrists around shoulder height, palm facing down. Again let the wrists lead.

3. As you breathe out, retrace the circle, wrists leading down, to return the arms to the start position again describing a circle finishing palms upward.

4. Each complete breath counts as one exercise.

Fifth Posture (Fire)

Fire is said to relate to the kidneys and is repeated to left and right sides. Fire will eventually introduce you to spiral energy movement from leg to left/right side.

1. Rotate hands around, palms facing as if holding a 15 cm (6") ball at the top and bottom, right hand below left, elbows in a 'v' slightly below each hand.

2. Sinking the Kua a little (softening the left knee to pivot at the hip), allow the hands to move over the left hip.

3. As you breathe in, slowly expand the hands apart, pulling against an imaginary vertical spring (Qi).

4. As you breathe out, slowly compress the hands, pushing against the vertical spring. Do not touch the hands together.

5. Each complete breath counts as one exercise.

6. After completing several breaths, transfer back to a neutral stance carrying the ball, rotate the hands so that left hand is on the bottom and carry out the movement on the right side.

7. Breathing in and out, expand and compress the hands vertically as before.

8. Each complete breath counts as one exercise.

9. After completing several breaths, transfer back to a neutral stance carrying the ball, rotate the hands so that they are vertical, then place them to the Dan Tien.

Finishing

1. Gather Qi in the palms of your hands, lift slightly then invert the palms and push Qi down the legs, lowering the hands down to your sides.

2. Straighten the knees and stand up.

3. Step the legs in together and 'bounce' and flex the legs and feet. Walk around to release the build up of Qi.

Five Element Qi Gong As A Simple Form

The five movements described previously can be singularly joined together as a complete sequence (or form) and repeated at least 3 times to provide a gentle static exercise sequence. As a short introductory 'form', this will not only bring awareness and control of Qi, but will start to generate an awareness of smooth movement and demonstrate the philosophy of Yin & Yang.

Carry out the 5 movements as a continuous flowing sequence of single passes. If you tire with the static stance or your back hurts because your posture is tensing then straighten the legs and stay in this position until refreshed (or even stop and walk around), and then return to the soft knee posture when able.

1. Assume the Earth Movement.

2. Carry out the Metal Movement.

3. Carry out the Water Movement.

4. Carry out the Wood Movement.

5. Carry out the Fire Movement on both sides.

Repeat as many times as you want, then to finish:

6. Gather Qi in the palms of your hands, lift slightly then invert the palms and push Qi down the legs, lowering the hands down to your sides.

7. Straighten the knees and stand up.

8. Step the legs in together and 'bounce' and flex the legs and feet. Walk around to release the built up Qi.

A Few Basic Sun Style Movements

If you are learning Sun Style, the following few pages may be a help when your teacher is not around.

Sun style T'ai Chi is the style that I practise most, and the one that I always recommend for beginners, especially those who may have balance or arthritic problems.

Sun style T'ai Chi was the last major form style to be created. It has elements taken from other traditional T'ai Chi styles, plus elements of Ba Gua and Xing Yi martial arts, making it a more diversified form adaptable to mixed abilities and applications.

The form - often referred to as 'Nimble T'ai Chi' - is characterised by its upright stance, agile steps and powerful internal and external movements. Unlike Yang Style, generally whenever one foot moves forward or backward the other foot follows creating a flowing "lapping wave" effect. Easy on the knee joints, this form is particularly suitable for all age groups, and its therapeutic properties make it ideal for people with balance and joint problems. This attribute has been adopted by Dr Paul Lam who uses Sun form as the basis for his T'ai Chi for Health modified forms.

The generally accepted variants of Sun style hand form are:

- The original Sun 97 step Long Form devised by Sun Lutang in 1919 and a Sun 42 step Short Form created by Sun's daughter, Sun Jian Yun.

- A Sun 73 step Competition Form sequence devised by a Wu Shu committee for the first Asian games in 1991. This was based on the 97, with a few movements modified to test athletes' flexibility, stamina and control of balance.

- A traditional Sun 13 and 38 step Short Form by Professor Li Deyin (a member of the committee above).

- Dr Paul Lam's 'T'ai Chi For Arthritis'. This is a short form modified for health and age related support. It incorporates mirrored versions of some of the easier Sun style movements specifically to ensure that both sides of the body are equally and safely exercised.

Introductory Sun Form Movements

There are several 'short' Sun forms that are suitable for beginners. I prefer either Deyin 13 Step or Dr Paul Lam's 'Tai Chi for Arthritis'.

However to avoid having to pick a favourite to accompany this book, I have selected the following few movements from the traditional Sun style forms. The movements are the opening ones that are common to the 97, 42, 73 and Deyin 38 to which I have added *'Waving hands like clouds'* and *'Yin & yang becomes one'* (also common to all) The movements will 'sequence', and can be used as a simple personal practice form requiring a 2.5m (8ft) sideways length.

The following instructions and pictures are included to help beginners and also to act as an aide mémoire to those who may prefer images to words. They are NOT intended to teach the intricacy of the movement - that's your teacher's job!

Please note: Elderly, less mobile beginners or those with balance or joint problems are advised initially to carry out the turning movements using a conventional step-around type movement rather than the heel/toe pivots described.

1. Commencement Form

Focus, relax and root. Shift weight to the left and soften the knee. Pivot right foot on its heel to angle your body to the left diagonal.
Immediately roll weight back to the right foot, lifting the left heel and lifting the hands up and out from the Dan Tien with the palms facing.

An easier alternative for the less mobile is not to rotate the right foot but to stay facing front and just soften knees a little as you lift.

2. **Step round to Leisurely Tie the Coat** *(Tucking in the Robes)*

   Sink weight back to right and withdraw hands to Dan Tien. Step with the left foot extending arms back out.

   Pivoting on right toe/left heel, turn to right, circling hands horizontally around right shoulder, right palm up, guided by left. Sitting back on left leg, lift right toe as hands traverse the circle, then move weight to right foot and push right hand forward. Follow through step with left foot.

3. **Opening Hands**

   Turn to front pivoting on left toe and right heel. Open the hands.

4. **Closing Hands**

   Close the hands, shifting weight to right.

5. Single Whip Right

Step left leg out so that toes point approximately 30 degrees, palms facing out to the front at shoulder height. Transfer weight to left leg, opening hands to the 'Single Whip' looking right.

6. The Big Bird Spreads Wings

Part the Hands: Step right leg in to an empty stance, while circling left hand to forehead and right hand to Dan Tien, fingers pointing down.
Spread the Wings: Lift right hand in a slight outward curve to face height, palm downwards, whilst lowering left hand to hip and sinking weight down on left.
Push: Step right leg forward with follow-through left foot as you push both hands centrally forward. *Don't over-extend arms.*

7. Opening Hands

Open the hands.

8. Closing Hands

Close the hands, shifting weight to right.

9. Turning Left and Brush Knee

Lift left heel, look at right hand over shoulder. Step out to left placing left heel down to start turn to the left. As you step-turn, push the right hand forward 'brushing' left hip (knee) with left hand.
Follow-through step with right foot.

10. Playing the Lute (left)

Step back right foot and withdraw right arm and extend left arm to sit back with follow-through 'empty' stance on left leg to 'Play the Lute'.

11. Advancing Steps - Sliding Hands

Advance forward two linked steps.
As you step left foot, slide right hand forward and as you step right foot, slide left hand.
There is no follow-through step when advancing.

Chapter 12 *Introductory Practice* 125

12. Parrying & Punching Over

Continuing with a further advance step with left foot, left arm parrying across towards the right hip and right arm making fist to punch over the parrying left wrist. Follow-through right step as you complete the punch.

13. Closing up to Embrace Tiger & Push the Mountain

Shift weight back to right foot, withdrawing left foot to an 'empty' stance. As you sit back, pull hands to waist, rotating them so palms are up

Lift the hand upwards a little and rotate to push forward, stepping left foot with follow-through right foot.

14. Opening Hands

Pivot turn back to front on right toe / left heel. Open the hands.

15. Closing Hands

Close the hands, shifting weight to left.

16. Turning Right and Brush Knee

Lift right heel, look at left hand over shoulder. Step out to right placing right heel down to start turn to the right. As you step-turn, push the left hand forward 'brushing' right hip (knee) with right hand and follow-through step with left foot.

17. Leisurely Tie the Coat *(Tucking in the Robes)*

Left hand lowers downwards. Step back left foot, withdrawing right foot to 'empty' stance and pulling arms down to left hip to 'roll back'.
Step right foot forward *(no follow-through step)*. Sitting back on left leg, circle hands horizontally around right shoulder, guided by left hand, right palm up. Lift right toe as the hands circle, then move weight to right and push right hand forward with left foot follow-through step.

18. Turning to Open and Close Hands

Pivot turn back to front on left toe / right heel. Open the hands.

19. Close Hands

Close the hands, shifting weight to right.

20. Single Whip (Right)

As per movement 5, step left leg out, palms to the front at shoulder height. Transfer weight to left, opening the hands and looking right.

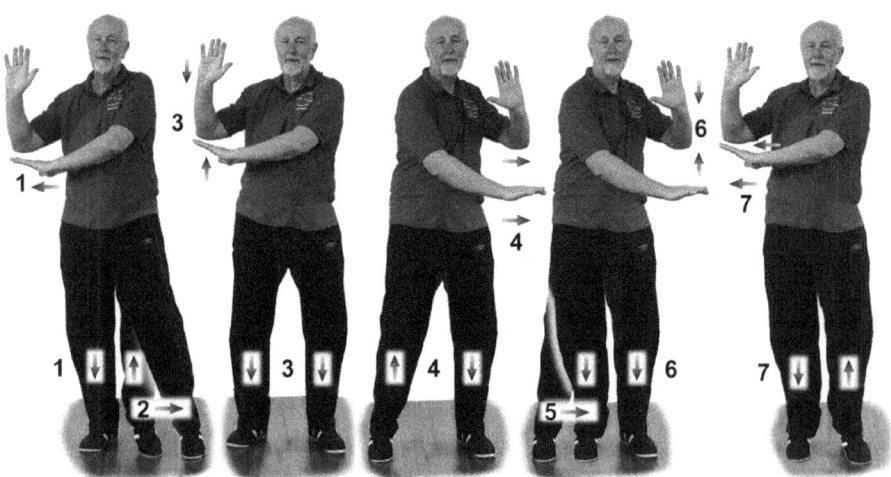

21. Wave Hands Like Clouds (stepping 3 steps to left)

(1) Transfer weight to right, and step left foot to right in 'empty' stance, and bring left hand to right elbow. (2) Step left foot back out to left side. (3) Swap hand position (left up, right down) shifting weight to both legs. (4) Carry hands and transfer weight to left leg, holding vertical position. (5) Step right foot back in to left. (6) Swap hand position (right up, left down) shifting weight to both legs.

(7) Carry hands and transfer weight to right, holding vertical position. You will be back to your original stance. *Repeat two more times*.

Chapter 12 Introductory Practice   129

22. Opening Hands and Closing Hands

Step left foot to root on both legs facing front. Open the hands.

23. Closing Hands

Close the hands, shifting weight to left.

24. Yin & Yang Becomes One and Closing Form

Step right foot back, whilst crossing right fist in front of left. Rotate the left fist downwards and outwards around the right fist to block, while slightly lifting and pressing left heel into the ground.

Withdraw left foot, lower hands and straighten the body to complete the form.

A Few Basic Yang Style Movements

This 8 Step (10) step Yang form was developed in 1999 by T'ai Chi Masters from the official Chinese Sports Council.

Sometimes referred to as 10 step (to include the commencing and closing movements), this is a compact Yang form that teaches the primary constituent movements of Yang style T'ai Chi. It is an ideal way for beginners to learn Yang style movement and posture. The form takes around 4 minutes to complete and has limited sideways steps to left and right making it ideal for home practice as it can be performed in a small 2 metre space.

The 8 Step Yang Form

The following instructions and pictures are included to help beginners and also to act as an aide mémoire to those who may prefer images to words. They are NOT intended to teach the intricacy of the movement - that's your teacher's job!

Preparation - Earth Rising, Heaven Descending

Step left foot out to the side.

Lift and lower hands, palms facing down, wrists leading, and sink to a Horse Stance.

Right   Left

1. **Repulse Monkey** *(Forward facing - Right and Left push).*

   Sink Kua to right. Look at right hand and push forward while circling left hand upwards. and push back to front.

   Keep the movement flowing and sink Kua to left and repeat for left hand push.

   Movements are forward facing, no step.

Left   Right

2. **Brush Knee & Twist Step** *(Left and Right side)*

   Step-turn to left side brushing knee, forming left bow stance and pushing right hand forward. Heel & toe pivot turn back to front.

   Repeat right side. Return to front.

Left   Right

3. Part Wild Horse's Mane *(Left and Right side)*

Hold ball, step-turn to left side, left bow stance. Push weight down on right leg and circle left arm upwards looking at the palm.
Hold ball as you heel/toe turn through front, and repeat to right side.
Hold ball as you heel/toe turn to front for movement 4 - 'Cloud Hands'.

to Left *(as illustrated)* then reverse the steps back to the **Right**

4. Wave Hands Like Clouds *(Stepping to Left & then back to Right)*

(1) Weight to right, hands on right side from the previous movement.
(2) Step left foot out. (3, 4) Carry weight & hands left.
(5) Step in right. (6, 7) Swap hands. Carry weight & hands back right.
(8) Step left foot out. (9,10,11) Swap hands. Carry weight & hands left.
(12) Step in right. (13) Swap hands.
Mirror the steps back to right ready for movement 5 - 'GoldenRooster'.

Left   Right

5. Golden Rooster Stands On One Leg
(Forward facing - standing on Left and then Right leg)
Weight to left leg and lift right leg and arm.
Transfer weight to right leg and lift left leg and arm.

Right   Left

6. Kick *(Forward facing - Right and Left kick).*
Transfer weight to left leg and kick with right.
Transfer weight to right leg and kick with left.
Ideally this is a full Heel Kick. However, for beginners or those less able, a small lift or toe point is fine.

7. Grasp The Swallow's Tail *(Right side)*

Complete the four part movement *(Peng, Lu, Ji, An)* to right side: (1) Ward Off, (2) Roll Back, (3) Press, (4 & 5) Push.

Step-turn to right. Heel-turn to return to front.

Grasp the Swallow's Tail *(Left side)*

Repeat the four movements to left side.

Chapter 12 Introductory Practice 135

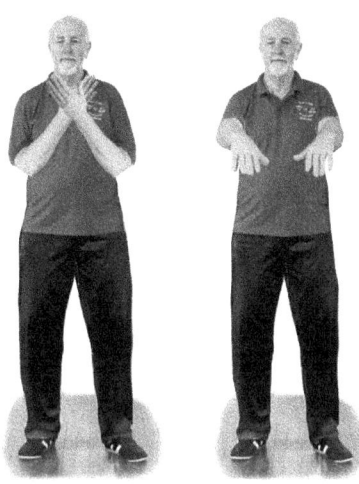

8. Cross Hands

Push the arms out to the side, then scoop up to cross in front of the upper chest.

Open arms outward, turning the hands palms down and lower them, sinking to a Horse Stance.

Closing Movement

Drop hands to sides, step left foot in and straighten upwards.

Chapter 13
An Introduction To Zhan Zhuang

A book written to introduce beginners to T'ai Chi and Qi Gong would not be complete without reference to basic Zhan Zhuang.

Standing Like A Tree

If you ever observe a large group of people in China practising T'ai Chi in a park or public square, you'll probably find that, unlike in formal or display sessions, you will see a multiplicity of T'ai Chi and Qi Gong styles being carried out as individuals exercise on their own oblivious to others around them.

If you study them more closely, you may see that some are just standing stationary in a fixed posture for maybe 10 minutes or longer, eventually moving but only to another static posture. Looking longer at these people, you may also detect a very slight gentle swaying movement in their apparent rigidity.

These people are almost certainly practising a Qi Gong called Zhan Zhuang *(pronounced Jan Jong)* which has an accepted translation of 'Standing Like a Tree'. Imagine a tree - a tree with a solid trunk and strong, spreading branches, deep roots firmly embedded in the ground - a tree that appears immovable, yet when observed over a few years is growing from the inside.

One of the modern masters of Zhan Zhuang, Lam Kam Chuen, says:

> *When you stand, you are like a tree. You are growing from within.*
> *Your feet, like roots, draw power from the earth.*
> *Your body, like the trunk, is perfectly aligned.*
> *You are unmoving, strong.*
> *Your head is open to the heavens like the crown of the tree.*
> *You rest calmly, the universe within your mind.*

Zhan Zhuang is one of the few major Chinese exercise routines that involves no direct physical movement, yet combines all the elements of an ideal whole body exercise: the physical development of health, strength, muscle tone and posture control combined with internal calmness, philosophy and personality enhancement.

In modern China research into its effects has endorsed its benefits, and as such it is used extensively in Chinese medical therapy in hospitals and clinics for the treatment of a wide range of conditions, and also by serious students of many internal martial arts (not only T'ai Chi), where it is used to develop full physical and mental body control. Originally a martial arts 'secret', it is now practised by increasing numbers of people throughout China and also forms part of the training of some of the country's top athletes to provide increased blood circulation, greater breath capacity and enhanced muscle tone.

Its creation is attributed to the health methods used by Daoists. In more recent centuries, martial artists adopted Zhan Zhuang to create a superior exercise, often devoting up to 50% of their practice time to it. The postures stimulate the flow of your body's internal energy *Qi*. Once you have overcome any physical fatigue, holding the positions helps you to mentally relax in meditation, while at the same time, building up your muscle power and resilience and improving posture. This regulates the flow of vital energy by helping your whole system to relax while strengthening the ability of your body and mind to withstand stress.

Despite the tremendous energy that it is capable of eventually generating, it can be practised by anyone, of any age, anywhere, without special equipment or clothing, and can be adapted for a seated position. Although long time periods are hard to maintain at first, with progressive practising and a little patience, once you begin to feel the benefits, you will find that Zhan Zhuang can be a treasure for life.

Before You Begin Zhan Zhuang

I have decided to include instruction for this Qi Gong in my book for beginners for potential use in the early development of posture and stance awareness. Adopting basic Zhan Zhuang will be invaluable for those intending to progress to higher levels of T'ai Chi. I have also found that many who are recovering from or managing spinal problems can often benefit from including this in their practice.

The postures shown here are a basic sequence of five. Some teachers may use just one posture (normally posture 2) or progress the sequence in a different order; others may introduce other static postures, normally drawn from animal stances or from your T'ai Chi form postures.

Please be aware that the simple postures shown here can be very demanding when carried out correctly, even if only just for a few minutes, and it is recommended that before attempting any Zhan Zhuang, absolute beginners wait until they are happy with some basic Qi Qong and form, and have started to appreciate basic posture and movement, preferably under the guidance of a teacher.

Important Practice Tips Before You Start

WARNING: In the early weeks of practice, holding a stance too long or incorrectly can cause muscle fatigue and/or shaking. Normally the recommendation when it is used as a health aid is 30 seconds to 2 minutes per posture, progressing gradually to 15 minutes, however serious traditional martial art students may eventually spend 2 hours per posture! **BUT PLEASE DON'T YOU OVERDO IT!**

- Ideally choose a calm tranquil place to practise.

- Some beginners may initially experience severe muscle fatigue and trembling. With some this can happen within just a few minutes and can be very worrying. You perspire, your calm breathing becomes erratic and your mind says stop - SO DO STOP. This is why you need to progressively build up the duration of your practice and not try to push yourself too hard in the early weeks.

- My recommendation for beginners to Zhan Zhuang is that the period for holding a posture is initially 30 seconds to 2 minutes, progressing gradually over many weeks to 5 to 15 minutes. It is far better to start learning with a single posture using a very short time period, progressively increasing the time over a few weeks, as this way you develop stamina and start to fully learn and experience the effects of this 'static exercise', rather than negating your effort by becoming fatigued and stressed. In these early weeks you work only on a single posture and once the allotted time period is expired, the exercise is not normally repeated in that session. Once you have started to develop the physical stamina required by only working on one posture at a time and are comfortable with for example 5 minutes of a posture, tick that one off and move to another next session.

- Eventually, after a few months, when you have accustomed your body to each position you will be ready for a five movement sequence. When you are practising the sequence, initially time each posture stance to a fifth of the total time period that you have held each movement.
Let's say that you have practised each posture using single 10 minute sessions. Now practise a sequence of five postures for 2 minutes per posture stance. This way you are still only standing for the same overall time of 10 minutes that you had achieved with each single posture.
In future sessions progressively extend the time for each posture in the sequence, thus extending your overall practice time.

- *How can you measure how long you are standing in a posture?*
You can always watch a clock or use a kitchen timer, but one of the best ways and more befitting the meditative nature of Zhan Zhuang, is to count your breath cycles - typically fifteen slow, deep in and out breaths will take around a minute. This is only a guide as not everyone breathes at the same rate, and as you progress with T'ai Chi and Qi Gong, your breathing will get deeper and slower.

- Feet should be about shoulder width apart, knees soft, spine & coccyx hanging down, neck and head relaxed, body as if it is suspended by a piece of string. Your mouth slightly open, ideally breathing through nose if you can. Imagine that you are sitting on the edge of a large soft balloon. There should be a small balloon under each armpit and a larger one between the knees. The fingers should also be held loosely apart by a mini balloon (but not splayed out or rigid). Depending upon the posture additional 'balloons' may support your elbows or hands.

- When you are standing, be as quiet as possible. Just be where you are and be very still. Feel calm and happy. You will hopefully experience a feeling of deep meditation. Eventually you will feel as if your body is expanding naturally, both physically and mentally.

- After a period of settling down into a posture, start observing how your body keeps balance. Gradually you will become aware of small movements of your body. At the beginning, there is tendency to correct for this by a physical movement such as leaning backward or forward. DO NOT try to control your involuntary movements this way as it defies the basic requirement of a straight back and impairs circulation.

Instead, imagine standing in a warm stream and feel your body swaying as if moved by slow waves. Let your whole body sway as one unit and eventually you will develop the ability to gently counter and control these movements by applying subtle internal resistance to 'give and take' the movement. You do this by modifying the tension in different muscles in the legs, arm and back to compensate and control. At first, this may feel uncomfortable as it increases the load on your entire body; nevertheless it is correct, and is one of the key factors in understanding the essence of deeper application of T'ai Chi energy sensing and movement.

So now you are aware of the basic intentions and are ready to start to practise and enjoy Zhan Zhuang...........

The Postures Of Zhan Zhuang

Although shown standing, the postures can be modified for sitting.

Commencing

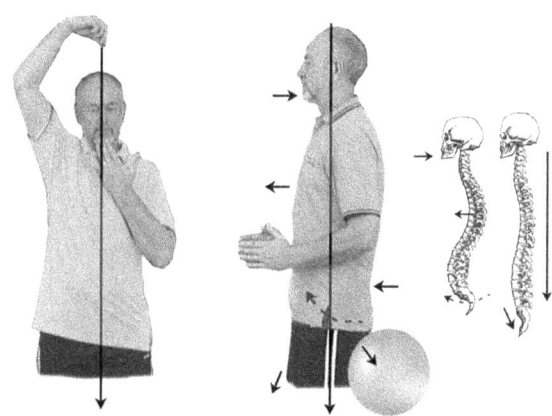

Carry out a simple warm up and then adopt the basic standing T'ai Chi posture:

1. Feet slightly apart - about shoulder width; head up - as if pulled up by an invisible string; chin slightly pulled in; fingers slightly apart and slightly curved; tail-bone dropped down - as if sitting against a balloon; knees have no tension - soft and slightly forward.
DO NOT lean forward or backward.

2. Breath deeply (ideally through the nose), cleanse the mind, and think and focus on the posture(s) about to be carried out.

3. Ideally use a slow deep breath counting:
 'In': *one, two, three, four.*
 'Out': *one, two, three, four.*

142   *Simplifying T'ai Chi*

First Posture - Wu ji (the primary energy posture)

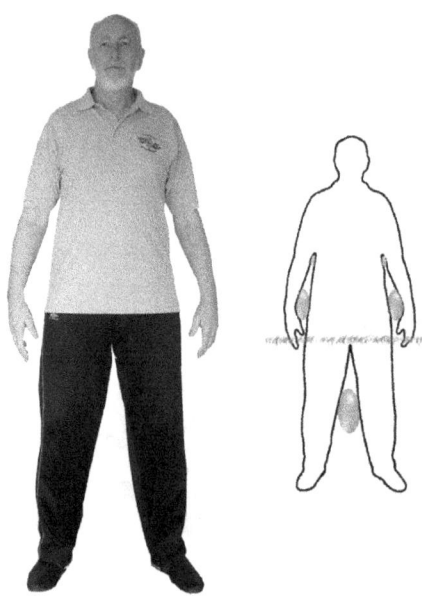

This basic posture concept has already been used as a simple Qi Gong on page 111. Now we intend to hold this posture for a much longer period.

1. Hold the hands by the side of the hips palms facing inward. Imagine that you are sitting on the edge of an imaginary balloon and that there is a small balloon between your legs and between your lower forearms and your body, and even smaller ones under your armpits and between your fingers.

2. Focus on sinking Qi to the Dan Tien whilst breathing slowly and deeply. Seek out any tensions in your body and relax them by readjusting muscle use *(song)*.

3. Imagine that you are standing waist deep in a gentle current of water that is moving past your hands. Use the flow of this current to gently stabilise your body.

Second Posture - Embracing the Tree

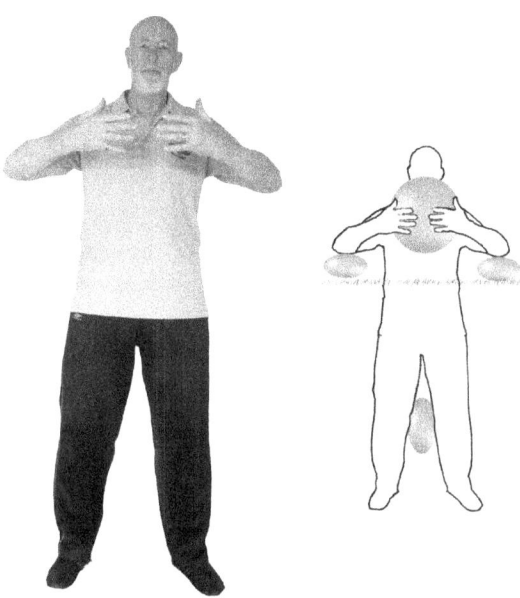

Here imagine that you are hugging a tree. This posture is often used by those who are practising Zhan Zhuang using only one position.

1. Lift the hands to a position with the palms facing the chest at a height that puts the little fingertips level with the heart and the thumb tips with the top of the shoulder *(hands in alignment with the middle Dan Tien)*. Elbows and hands are away from the body as if you are holding a balloon gently against your chest.

2. Take care not to tension your shoulders but try not to drop or lift your elbows - imagine that the water you are standing in is midway up your chest and that your elbows are supported by an inflated balloon or cushion on the surface. If you press the elbows down the balloons will resist - if you lift your elbows up, the balloons will float away - learn to control them.

3. Don't hold your hands too far out or too far in towards your body.

4. Focus on breathing, and again readjust muscles to compensate for tension.

In the first posture described earlier, the stance is balanced and central with arms down at the sides of the body. The transition into the second posture consists of raising the arms up and holding them in front of you. This action shifts your centre of gravity slightly forwards, and unless you compensate for this shift you will feel unbalanced as if about to topple over. Learn to compensate by altering muscle tension rather than by just leaning back.

Third Posture - Holding the Belly

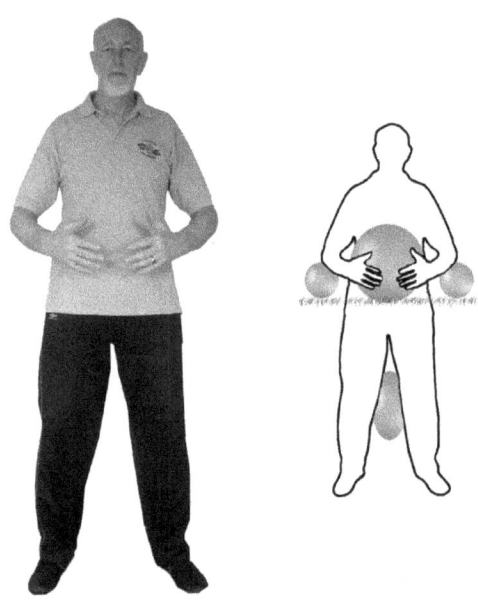

As you slowly lower your hands into this posture, again appreciate the subtle difference in the core muscle tension in your back as you compensate for the change in arm position.

1. Lower your hands, palm still facing inwards until your fingers point at the Dan Tien and towards opposite knees. Imagine that you are holding a large balloon gently against your stomach, but not so hard as to distort its shape or burst it.

2. Don't hold your hands too far out or too far in towards your body.

3. Let your elbows adopt a natural 'soft' position. Again try not to drop them too low or raise them too high - imagine that the water you are standing in is up to your hips and that the balloon that you are holding and your elbows are floating on the surface.

4. Focus on your breathing and ensure relaxation *(song)*.

Fourth Posture - Standing in the Current

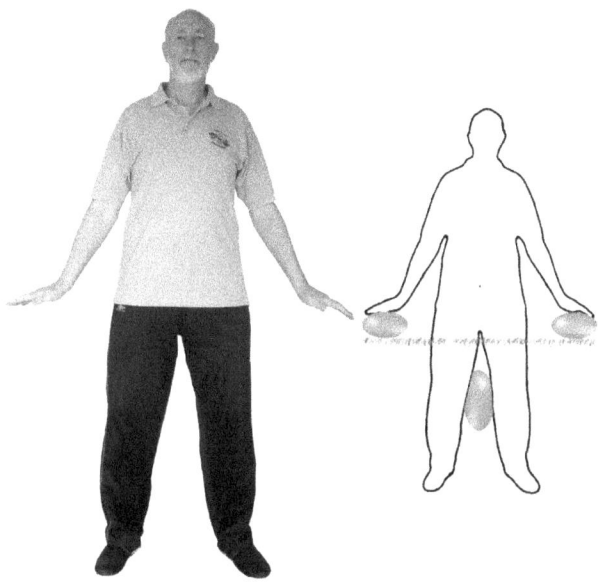

This time the hands are moved out to the side of the body. As before note how the simple change in posture subtly changes the muscle use.

1. Soften your knees a little further and move your hands out to the side about 9" (20-25cms) from hips, palms facing downward.

2. Imagine that the water you are standing in is up to your hips and that there are small balloon or planks of wood under your hands. The current will try to move the balloons or planks, but by gently pressing down you keep them in position.

3. Focus on your breathing and releasing tension *(song)*.

Fifth Posture - Holding a Ball in Front of the Face

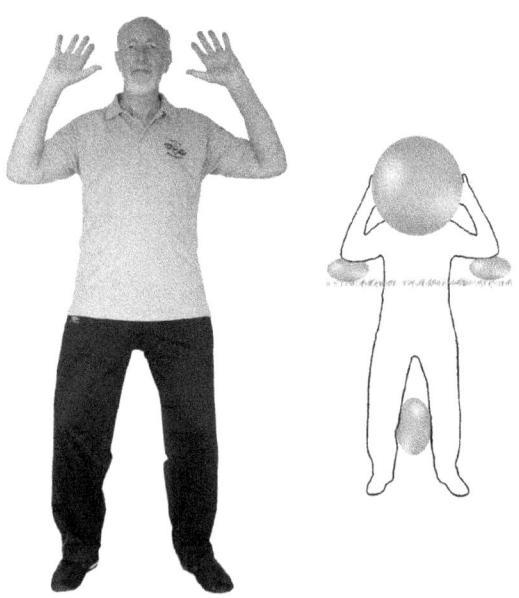

1. With the knees softened as in Posture 4 (and lower still if you can manage softer knees), lift your arms so that the hands are shoulder width apart and held at face height (but only 3-5 cms in front of the face - you should just be able to see your thumbs and first fingers through the corner of your eye). Palms face forwards (as if about to score with an oversized basket-ball), with your thumbs approximately level with your ears and your fingertips with the top of your head.

2. Find a 'balanced' position with no shoulder tension. Again try not to drop your elbows too low or lift them too high. This time you should imagine you are supporting a large balloon in front of your face and that you are about to push it over a high wall or are about to score with your basket-ball. Your elbows are again supported by balloons or cushions floating on the surface of water which is now back up to your chest.

3. Focus on your breathing and releasing tension *(song)*.

Finishing the Session

1. Gather Qi in the palms of your hands, lift slightly then invert the palms and push Qi down the legs, lowering the hands down to your sides.

2. Slowly straighten the knees and stand up. Step the legs in together and 'bounce' and flex your legs and feet and then walk around and enjoy the moment.

Sequencing the Basic Postures

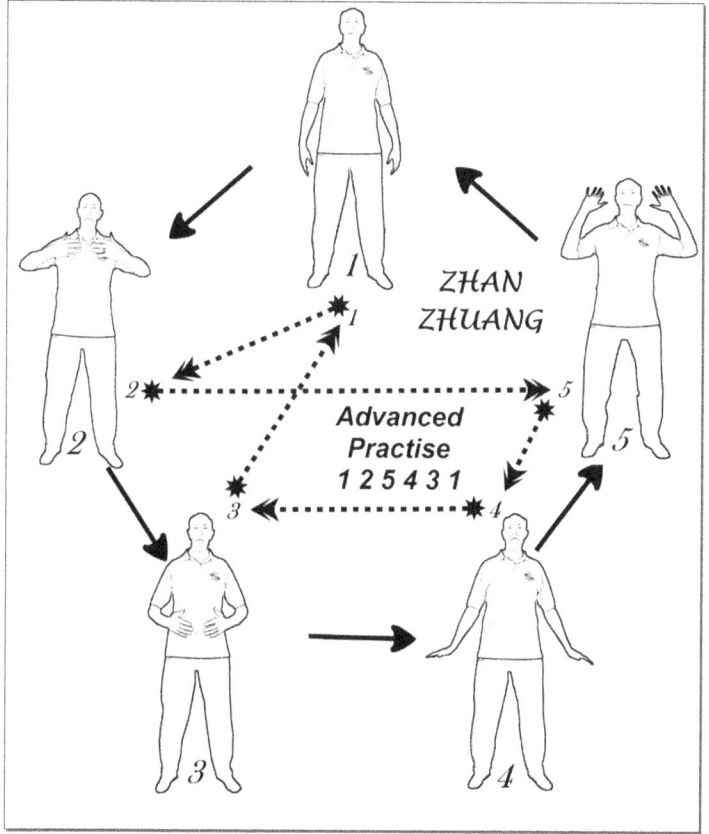

Simple Zhan Zhuang Learning and Advanced Sequences

The order that the basic postures are practised in can vary. The picture above illustrates the usual sequence to use when you start learning Zhan Zhuang and compares it to one of the sequences that is often chosen in traditional teaching.

The initial learning sequence follows the order illustrated in the instructional text, **1-2-3-4-5-1**, which alternates lowered and raised arm postures.

The traditional sequence shown as an alternative in the diagram swaps over posture 3 and 5, changing the practice order to **1-2-5-4-3-1**.
This sequence is much more demanding for the beginner as it puts the most wearying raised arm posture (5) immediately after the raised arm stance (2), and does not give you the opportunity to lower your arms and 'rest' them using the lowered arm postures (3 & 4).

Chapter 14
A Potted History of T'ai Chi

Many people starting their T'ai Chi journey are amazed when told that the "ancient" art they are learning only came into prominence in China in the nineteenth century.

Most books about T'ai Chi contain a similar history of its evolution and so I'll include my short summary based on various researched versions, but make no claim for definitive accuracy. If you find controversy, blame it on 'Chinese whispers'!

T'ai Chi has Taoist roots and T'iyu (Taoist Physical Culture) has been handed down for over 10,000 years. The traditional origins of T'ai Chi are however assumed to be based on the principles reputedly practised by Taoist monks around 1000 BC.

Research indicates that the next phase of the art may have begun in the Tang dynasty (618 - 906 AD). However a Taoist monk named Chang San-Feng (born in the Sung dynasty around 1247) is generally regarded as the initial founder of T'ai Chi. It is said that he saw a crane attacking a snake and was inspired by the soft and yielding movement as the supple snake out-manoeuvred and overcame the hard-beaked crane.

This may be the accepted origination of 'soft' martial arts, but in reality the term T'ai Chi and the forms that we practise today have their roots only a few centuries ago in the Chen family, and its transfer outside the family to a man called Yang Lu-Ch'an (1799-1872).

It is therefore more correct to say that our T'ai Chi originates from the Chen family style which lost its secrecy around 170 years ago, and to say that today's other traditional styles (Yang, the two Wu styles and Sun) owe their origins and key disciplines to the original Chen style.

Over the past century the martial face of these traditional styles has been changed through different teachers so that the practice disciplines now range from true martial defensive forms to the modified forms practised for health and posture control. Many Masters and teachers have appeared, some directly lineaged from respected Chinese masters or from those that spread the art from Asia in the 1950's, while others are indirectly taught, but all have contributed to ensuring that T'ai Chi in all its guises now flourishes in most areas and communities around the world.

We are lucky that many more respected teachers - modern Masters - now work throughout the western world. Also many original highly respected Chinese teachers and their families now practise here. One of many is Professor Li Deyin's daughter and her husband who run a Taiji Institute in the UK, and from whom the author feels privileged to have received some of his instruction.

No matter what level you are learning, with the help of a good teacher your own goals (and more) will be achieved.

If you want to find out a little more about the origins of the style that you are practising, then read on.

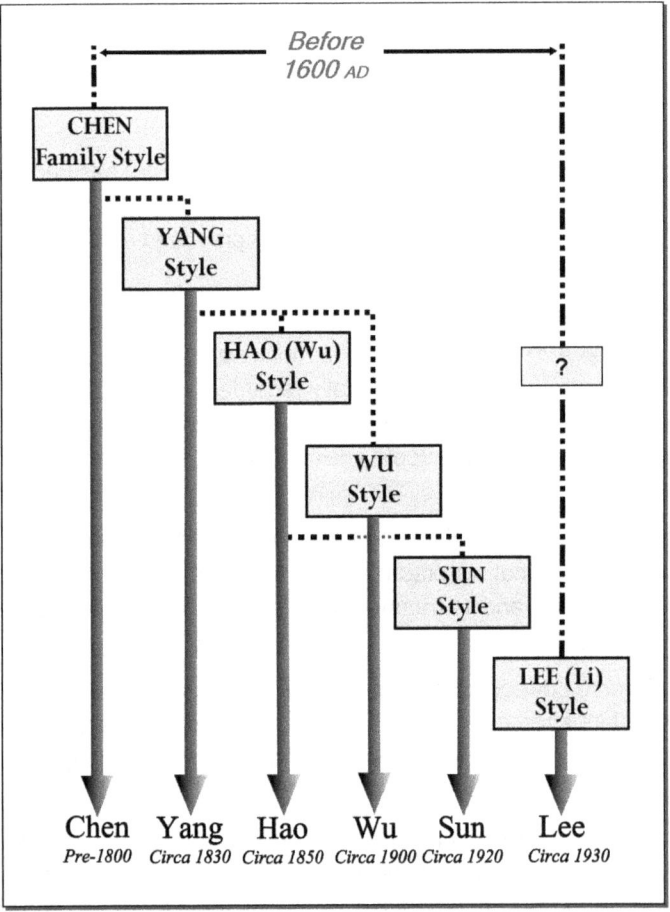

Evolution Dependency of the Major Classical T'ai Chi Styles

Chen Style

Although the art is based on Taoism and various older martial arts, it was first reported as being taught in strict secret as a discipline in its own right, to members of the Chen family living in a small village in Hopeh Province in the mid-1700s. By the early 1800s T'ai Chi was at its zenith as a fighting art, and the Chen style was well established. It was still though taught only to members of the Chen family. (In this context the term 'Family' is usually accepted as referring to a community or village.) This peak of Chen skill is attributed to the 14th generation and 6th grandmaster Chen Chang-Hsin *Chen Changxing* (1771-1853).

Because of its pedigree Chen style displays many martial disciplines. It has a low wide stance *(large frame - illustrated here by Chen Fake 1887-1957)* and incorporates fast and slow movements performed with both internal *Qi* and expulsive *Jin* energy. Compact *(short frame)* variants do exist but are not so commonly seen.

Chen form still remains a traditional style of T'ai Chi, often taught as a serious martial art to this day, and is sometimes selfishly referred to by some as the only 'true' T'ai Chi.

Yang Style

T'ai Chi's break from secrecy is normally attributed to a man named Yang Lu-Ch'an. who created the style that has since become the most popular one taught around the world. The story attributed to the creation Yang style T'ai Chi is as follows:

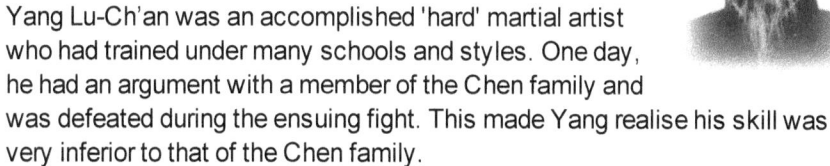

Yang Lu-Ch'an was an accomplished 'hard' martial artist who had trained under many schools and styles. One day, he had an argument with a member of the Chen family and was defeated during the ensuing fight. This made Yang realise his skill was very inferior to that of the Chen family.

He practised hard and asked for a return match, only to be humiliated yet again. At this point he recognised the Chens' superiority and vowed to learn this style for himself, only to discover that it was exclusive to the Chen family living in the Chen Chia Kou village. He also discovered that the Chen who defeated him was the nephew of the grandmaster Chen Chang-Hsin.

He knew that he would never be accepted to train with them and so decided to 'steal' the art from the family. He disguised himself as an almost blind beggar (also apparently making himself temporarily dumb by swallowing hot coals) and visited the Chen master hoping for sympathy. It worked, and he was employed as a servant in the household and soon became trusted and gained access to the inner sanctum of the family home.

Here he spied on the Chen family practice, and with his experienced martial art background he was able to copy and secretly learn them for himself. One night, as Yang secretly practised, he suddenly found himself being observed by the senior Chen master, and feared that he would be executed immediately.

To his surprise, the master merely said, 'Do you think I did not realise you were spying on us when we were practising? I allowed you to watch because I wanted to see how serious you were and how well you would benefit from the instruction. If you had shown neither interest nor skill, I would have killed you myself.' He then tapped Yang three times on the head and walked away.

From that day, Yang visited the master at three in the morning for instruction and then worked as a servant during the day so that no one higher up in the Chen family would know that he was receiving secret instruction.

Eventually the master explained that he had deliberately broken the family traditions because he had realised that by restricting the art to family, the effectiveness of T'ai Chi would eventually decline in vitality. With no-one to challenge outside the family, there would not be much incentive to practise well or to introduce new techniques, since even the poorest of them were far better than most practitioners from other schools of martial art.

He reasoned that if he taught a skilled outsider, he would ensure that the essence of T'ai Chi would not be lost to the world. T'ai Chi would remain vigorous and fresh as not only would it be practised by more people, but the family members would have to maintain their own standards. This tradition of selecting dedicated, deserving students to expand the art has persisted ever since.

Within the Chen family it was an established fact that, during competition, none of the younger members were able to defeat the older masters. It was assumed that this was because the master had so much more experience and practice, and by showing that proficiency to a younger opponent it indicated his years of practising, and that age did not impair ability.

Then one day Yang's teacher announced to the family 'If I can produce someone younger than myself who has acquired sufficient skill to defeat all of you, what would you all have to say?' After discovering that the proposed champion was in fact the servant, one after another, members of the Chen family challenged and were beaten by him. Feelings turned to anger as they realised that not only had an outsider been trained, but he had also learnt so well. They felt cheated and betrayed.

The senior Chen master then announced 'Yang Lu-Ch'an should go out and teach the world. If you fail to continue to practise well, you will then soon meet others who will be better than you. I have deliberately broken tradition by teaching an outsider to ensure that the knowledge of our art will not die, but will blossom and develop'.

Yang then left the Chen family to move on and establish a reputation and attract students. He wandered all over Hopeh Province, taking on all challengers for the next three years and was never defeated in any of his bouts. He further developed his own style and became known as 'Unbeatable Yang', and the name that he called his martial art system, T'ai Chi Chuan (Grand Ultimate Fist), has become the generalisation term for all subsequent styles of martial art T'ai Chi.

Around the mid-1800s Yang went to Beijing and started a school of T'ai Chi. Here he associated with two other 'soft' or 'internal' martial art schools Hsing I *(Xing Yi)* and Pa Kua *(Bagua)*. Together they challenged, defeated and expelled all other style schools from the city. For a long time after, only these three different martial art disciplines were taught there.

After Yang's death in 1872, his version of T'ai Chi Chuan, which we now refer to as Yang Style, was taught and passed down, mainly by members of his family who, over the years formalised standardised form taking typically 15-20 minutes to complete (usually referred to now as 'Long Yang', '108 Yang', 'Yang 120 Form', etc.).

Like its Chen roots, Yang style retained a wide and open stance *(large frame),* but its practice appears more flowing and slow. This can be attributed to Yang's third grandson, Yang Cheng-Fu 1883-1936 *(pictured here),* who has become one of the best known 'Yang family' teachers after he wrote books on the style published in 1931 and 1934. It is this 'gentler' movement that has tended to epitomise T'ai Chi as a meditative exercise and helped to increase its popularity worldwide. This fact however must not be allowed to belie its effectiveness as a serious martial art.

More upright *(small frame)* and fast variants of the form do exist which having medium to high stances and more compact movements, are suitable for close-quarters techniques. One such is the form created around 1950 by a master named Chen Man Ch'ing (1902-1975). *Don't be confused by his name - he was not a member of the Chen family.* His study lineage was from Yang's grandson, Yang Cheng-Fu.

With his master's agreement he introduced a major change to shorten the form to a 37 part one that now bears his name. This 'simplified' version was created to be shorter to teach to those less experienced in martial arts, but should never be considered as easier. It is definitely Yang style, but has less repetition and a deeper essence and is performed with a more upright and less expansive stance *(medium/short frame)*.

Around 1964 Cheng Man Ch'ing took his T'ai Chi to New York and introduced it to America, where his form became widely practised and established as one of the key Yang style forms.

Also, in the 1970's, a Norwegian lady, Gerda Geddes was instrumental in introducing T'ai Chi to the UK. With no martial background she taught long (108) Yang form purely for its health and physical benefits.

The first half of her life had taken her to China (where she first saw T'ai Chi performed as a morning exercise), and then on to Hong Kong. It was here in the mid-1950's that she started to study Yang form under Master Choy Hawk-Pang, a teacher who had also been a student of Yang Cheng-Fu. After the death of Master Choy she went on to learn from his son Choy Kam-Man.

Settling in England in the 60's she had many frustrating attempts to introduce T'ai Chi into London dance schools to provide corrective relief from the rigours of the dancer's intensive training. Eventually she established a foothold in a leading school and this led to more and more sessions both in London and all over the country, spreading the knowledge of T'ai Chi to thousands.

The version of long Yang form that she introduced and taught was the first form that the author learnt in depth and one that he still practises today.

The popular 24 movement Yang Short Form was created in 1956. It evolved when the Chinese Sports Committee brought a group of T'ai Chi teachers together to produce a briefer simplified form as exercise for the masses. They truncated the traditional Yang family form to 24 postures to create one which takes around six minutes to perform and still provides an introduction to all the essential elements whilst maintaining the intent of the original forms. An 8 posture version was developed in 1999.

The mass introduction of the 24 form and its subsequent expansion around the world have made this version of Yang form the most popular to be adopted, and it is said to account for 90% of the general T'ai Chi taught in the western world. Mostly it is taught well, though unfortunately, occasionally it can be taught badly with no depth or understanding. However, because of it's popularity, it is not too difficult for the beginner to find a good teacher to supplement the books and videos of accomplished modern Masters in order to learn it well.

Hao Style (Wu Hao Style)

Confusingly there are two styles that inherit the name Wu. The first which should really be referred to as Hao style, was created by Wu Yu Hsing, but is still is often referred to as Wu style. The second was created by Wu Chuan Yu and is the one that is now generally referred to as Wu style. Both creators were students of Yang Lu-Chan (founder of the Yang style).

The style of T'ai Chi, created by Wu Yu Hsing, (1812–1880) has a distinctive compact style *(small frame)* with small, subtle movements. The form itself concentrates on balance, sensitivity and internal Qi. Its name 'Hao/Wu style' derives from the school set up by a second generation student of Wu Yu Hsing named Hao Wei-Chen (1842-1920).

When compared to the other major styles it is rare to find this form practised today. However if you do get chance to see it demonstrated, the softening of Yang style form and similarities to Sun style form are very apparent. This is not surprising as Sun's creator Sun Lu Tang *(see later on page 156)* was trained in T'ai Chi by Hao Wei-Chen.

Wu Style

The style created by Wu Chuan Yu (1834-1902) is the one generally now referred to as Wu style and not the Wu Hao style, created by Wu Hsing (above).

The creator of the style was a Manchurian and also a student of Yang Lu-Chan (founder of the Yang style). His son, Wu Chien-Chaun (1870-1942), learnt from him, and around 1912 established the Wu style at the Beijing Sport Research Society by gradually refining his father's style. He later taught in Shanghai before moving to Hong Kong around 1938.

Originally, prior to around the start of the 20th century, traditional T'ai Chi styles were practised as a fast martial form. Because many people came to study in Beijing who had not previously done martial arts, many of the fast movements and jumps were taken out of the major styles of Chen and Yang form to be taught separately as application, leaving the more gentle, subtle, form which appears to flow like a lapping wave that we are more used to seeing today.

As the creator was trained in Yang style, Wu style has it roots based on this style, and initially was considered a variant of it, retaining the full fast form as well as having a slow form. Wu style primarily differs from Yang style by resequencing it, employing a narrower stance *(small frame)* and variations in some postures, the most obvious being the adoption of more severe waist bending and of a sloping stance in some of Yang's upright ones. *(The example illustrated appears to contradict most of the beginner's T'ai Chi maxims but is in reality still a fully structured martial stance with central-rooting, and must not be interpreted as an unstable leaning stance.)* Other changes give the form a compactness and an overall appearance of calm and smoothness from the beginning to the end of its practice.

Wu style, like Chen style, is usually adopted by those more interested with the martial aspects of T'ai Chi. However, as with any style, this does not preclude practising by any one who has a reasonable level of mobility.

When Wu Chien-Chaun died in 1942, his descendants continued to teach the style, expanding to Europe and the rest of the world over the succeeding decades. They are now into their 5th generation.

Sun Style

All of the major styles of T'ai Chi are founded upon similar principles, and are therefore related to one another historically as well as technically. Variations among the styles are primarily due to the differing backgrounds, experiences, and personalities of the founders, as well as the demands of the particular environment in which each style was created.

Sun style is no exception. Its uniqueness is due to the background of its founder, Sun Lu Tang, born Sun Fu Quan (1861-1933). A harsh childhood, high intelligence and a superior ability to master several styles of martial arts, including Xing Yi Quan, Bagua and latterly Wu Hao t'ai chi style, resulted in the creation of an extremely sophisticated yet practical T'ai Chi form that became Sun style.

He was in his fifties when he switched to developing his form, often alleged to have been because he was getting older and the anticipation that extreme movement was likely to become more difficult. The net result was the creation of a style that was the culmination of his past intense study, research and experience, and was the crowning achievement of his martial arts career.

Often called 'Nimble T'ai Chi', it inherits its spontaneous reactive movement from Xing Yi, movement and subtlety from Bagua, and characteristic upright stance and follow-through stepping from both. The form movements themselves are inherited from the Wu Hao T'ai Chi art and also contain elements of Qi Gong, Thus when it is performed it provides a close *(small frame)* sequence that is very suitable for both close combat and a health exercise.

Sun's influence on modern T'ai Chi was further established by the fact that he was the first person to author documents and books on the technique and philosophy of martial art and of his style. His first major work was published in 1915, and his book describing what is now known as Sun style T'ai Chi, containing photographs of every movement of a 97 step long form, was published in 1921. It has been translated to English and is still widely used today.

Sun's son Sun Cunzhou (1893-1963) continued to teach his form, as did his daughter, Sun Jian Yun (1914-2003), *pictured here,* and several western teachers have learnt from her. As with other styles, a shorter 42 step Short Sun Form was also created.

In 1991 a Sun 73 step Competition Form sequence was devised by the Chinese Wu Shu committee for the first Asian games. This was based on the traditional 97 step form, but had a few movements modified to test athletes' flexibility, stamina and control of balance. A traditional Sun 13 and 38 step Short Form has also been created by Professor Li Deyin (a member of the aforementioned Wu Shu committee).

Because of its upright stance with follow-through steps, Sun form is ideally adaptable for use as a health exercise form, especially for older novices and those with arthritic joints, as it maintains stability and encourages flexibility and more responsive movement. This characteristic has been adopted by Dr Paul Lam in his modified form 'T'ai Chi for Arthritis' now taught and used world-wide.

Over the years, Sun T'ai Chi has become the author's favourite T'ai Chi Style.

Lee Style

Many will add Lee *or Li* style to the major styles. Exponents of Lee style claim it to be the oldest form of T'ai Chi Chuan in existence, pre-dating Chen. Up until to 1934 it had always remained a family style, attributing its origination to a master called Ho-Hsieh Lee around 1,000 BC, implying that this style is nearly three thousand years old. As this was a time before there were any written records, we only have the oral tradition passed down from father to son to rely on.

Originally Ho-Hsieh Lee and his family lived just outside Beijing, and it was there, so the story is told, that he first started his practice and devised the first movements. When he was in his middle fifties he took his family and settled down in Wei Hei Wei, a fishing village about 200 miles east of Beijing, and they remained in that district through the centuries until the 1930s.

In 1933 the last in the line, Chan Kam Lee, the eldest of three children, came to London on business and started a small class in Holborn to keep himself and a few selected close friends fit. Here he met and adopted a young orphan, later to be known as Chee Soo, *(pictured right)* and passed the techniques on to him as he had no children of his own. This seeded Lee style in the UK. In the winter of 1953/4 Chan Kam Lee died in a severe coastal storm near Canton.

Thus it is through Chee Soo, his books and his students, that centuries of Lee style has been preserved, and continues to flourish around the world.

As with Sun style, Lee style is a higher stance *(short frame)*, balanced form. It is usually referred to as 'Yin and Yang T'ai Chi' as every part is in complete balance and harmony, or sometimes as the 'Square Yard T'ai Chi', because all the movements can be performed within around a square metre of floor space, enabling individual practising even in the smallest area.

Modified T'ai Chi for Health

Since 1970, several experienced T'ai Chi teachers have examined and researched the medical benefits that T'ai Chi can bring, and have devised modified forms that are based on the traditional movements and principles, but which are specifically targeted to aid and help manage chronic medical and age-related conditions.

This new generation of Masters includes Dr Paul Lam, an Australian Doctor of western medicine and a T'ai Chi competition gold medal winner and judge.

Since 1996 Dr Lam has trained thousands world-wide to teach his medically researched programs within the remit of the western health system. These forms, based on selected Sun and Yang style movements, include variants to assist the management of arthritis, osteoporosis, diabetes and several other potentially debilitating conditions.

The author of this book first met Dr Lam in 2001 and after training under him over many years, I acknowledge him as a key mentor in my own journey. It was Dr Lam's encouragement and guidance that first gave me the confidence to start to teach T'ai Chi to others, especially those with limited ability.

After experiencing my mother's health deteriorating rapidly with stroke and dementia, I produced my own modified program for the elderly based on T'ai Chi and Qi Gong movements. Since 2009 I have successfully used this program (which I call my *Twilight T'ai Chi*) in care home groups, many suffering from dementia-related illness, and plan to make it the subject of a future book.

Epilogue

"Of all the exercises, I should say that T'ai Chi is the best. It can ward off disease, banish worry and tension, bring improved physical health and prolong life. It is a good hobby for your whole life, the older you are, the better. It is suitable for everyone - the weak, the sick, the aged, children, the disabled and blind. It is also an economical exercise. As long as one has three square feet of space, one can take a trip to paradise and stay there to enjoy life for thirty minutes without spending a single cent".

T.T. Liang (Liang Tung-Tsai, 1900-2002)

"T'ai Chi Chuan, the great ultimate, strengthens the weak, raises the sick, invigorates the debilitated and encourages the timid."

Chen Man Ch'ing

Thank you for reading my book. Enjoy your T'ai Chi.

Trevor

Index

A

age-related problems 12, 16
age and ability 12
allegorical terminology 45
arm movement 61
arthritis 14

B

back
  pain 14
  posture 59
backward step 72
bagua (pa kua) 153
balance 104
best
  place 38
  practice 105
  time of the day 38
bow stance 74
breathing 85
  lower abdominal 86
  yang 86, 112
bubbling well 46

C

calmness 101
chan si jin 51, 92
Chee Soo 157-158
Chen Chang-Hsin 151
Chen Fake 151
chen family style 31, 151
Chen Man Ch'ing 32, 153, 161
chen style 93
chest 59
chi See qi (chi)
chi (qi) 19, 90
chi kung See qi gong
chidren's t'ai chi 35
clothes for t'ai chi 37
concentration 102
cooling down 110
cordination 103

D

dantien (tantien) 47, 87
Deyin-Professor Li 33
diabetes 15
do's and dont's 41
Dr Paul Lam 11, 33, 119, 157-158

E

eight energies 48, 98

empty
  and full 104
  mind 101
  stance 75
enjoyment 10, 105
exercise 7-9
external martial art 9
eyes 62

F

fa jin 49
falls prevention 15
fist 62
five elements 48, 94
  qi gong 112
five steps 48, 97
focus 101
foot movement 60
form 48
forward step 71
frame 49

G

Gerda Geddes 154
getting started 107

H

hand movement 61
hao style 155
hard martial art 9
health 11, 14
  benefits 14
health problems
  age related 16
  arthritis 14
  back pain 14
  diabetes 15
  falls prevention 15
  ms multiple sclerosis 16
  osteoporosis 15
  stress 16
Ho-Hsieh Lee 157
horse stance 69
hsing I (xing yi) 153

I

impromtu t'ai chi 38
internal martial art 9

J

jin 49, 97

K

kicks 79
  full 80
  knee lifts 80
  toe-points 79
knee movement 60

kua 50, 61, 81, 101
  sinking and opening 81

L

Lam Kam Chuen 137
lao gong (palace of toil) 47
Lee (Li) family style 157
leg movement 59
lessons
  after first 42
  finding a class/style 31
li (strength) 90
long yang form 31

M

martial art 7-8
meditation in motion 13
ming men (centre of vitality) 47, 67
mouth 62
movement 101
  arms 61
  balance 104
  concepts 11
  feet 60
  hands 61
  knee 60
  legs 59
  natural 103
  relaxed 102
  shoulders 61
  slow 102
  spontaneous 103
ms multiple sclerosis 16

O

origins 7
osteoporosis 15

P

pa kua (bagua) 153
pin yin 46
posture 56
  back 59
  breathing 85
  chest 59
  eyes 62
  head 58
  legs 59
  mouth 62
  of infinity 52, 65
  relaxed 57
  seated 68
  shoulders 61
  standing 65
  standing, sitting 57
Professor Li Deyin 33
punch 62
push hands 50

Q

qi (chi) 19, 47, 90
qi gong 19, 21-22, 35, 47
   basic seated 111
   five element 112
   flowing/moving 24
   meditative 24
   moving 24
   passive/static 24
   standing/sitting 24
   types 24

R

relaxed posture 57
rooted 103
   stance 69
   tree 55, 104

S

salute 39
seated t'ai chi 12
shen (spirit) 90
short yang form 31
shoulder movement 61
sifu, shifu 28
silk reeling (chan si jin) 51, 92
silk reeling qi gong 51, 92
sinking 103
six harmonies 51, 89, 101
   external three 81, 89
   internal three 90
soft martial art 9
song (sung) 51, 57, 142
spelling - western or pin yin 46
spiral energy 51, 92
stance 49
   transferring from low to high 83
standing like a tree (zhan zhuang) 53, 137-138, 141
sticky hands 50
stress 16
style 51
   choosing 31
Sun Jian Yun 33, 157
Sun Lu Tang 33, 156
sun style 32, 119, 156
   13 & 38 de yin short form 33, 119, 157
   42 step short form 119, 157
   73 step competition form 119, 157
   97 step long form 119, 157
   bow stance 74

T

t'ai chi (definition of) 52
T.T. Liang (Liang Tung-Tsai) 6, 29, 161
Tai Chi for Health by Dr Paul Lam 11, 33, 158
taiji, taijiquan 7, 19, 52
taoist 149
teacher 27-28
terminology 45
thirteen postures 48, 97
turns, turning 76
   heel & toe 77
   spin 79
   stepping 77
twilight t'ai chi 12

W

warming up 109
weight shift 68
wu
   hao style 155
   style 155
Wu Chuan Yu 155
Wu Hsing 155
wu style 31
wuji 52, 65

X

xing yi (hsing I) 153

Y

yang
   breathing 86, 112
Yang Chen-Fu 153
Yang Lu-Ch'an 31-32, 151
yang style 31, 151
   24 step short form 154
   8 step form 130, 154
   bow stance 74
   long (108) form 153
yawning 21
yi (mind, intent) 90, 102
yin and yang 53, 87, 104
yongquan 46

Z

zhan zhuang (standing like a tree) 53, 137-138, 141

www.ingramcontent.com/pod-product-compliance
Lightning Source LLC
Chambersburg PA
CBHW071207160426
43196CB00011B/2219